SHE

Primal Meetings with the Dark Goddess

Note to Readers

This workbook is for entertainment purposes only. It is not a substitute for medical, legal, or financial counsel. The authors and publisher assume no legal or moral liability for damages, losses, or other consequences of reader decisions subsequent to, or based upon, the contents and activities presented herein.

SHE

Primal Meetings with the Dark Goddess

Storm Constantine & Andrew Collins

Including Contributions From
Caroline Wise
Deborah Cartwright
Richard Ward
Maggie Jennings

Megalithica Books
Stafford England

SHE: Primal Meetings with the Dark Goddess
by Storm Constantine & Andrew Collins
© 2018 First edition

All essays and pathworkings © Storm Constantine and Andrew Collins, 2018 except for:

Deborah Cartwright – *Ashina: Grey She-Wolf*, and *Meeting Ashina*. © 2018
Maggie Jennings – *Meeting Sekhmet* and *Meeting Nephthys*. © 2018
Richard Ward – *Erzuli Danto: Mother of Freedom* & *Meeting Erzuli Danto*. © 2018
Caroline Wise – *Archetypal Bad Girls and Femmes Fatales*, *Meeting Black Annis*, *Meeting Hel* and *Meeting Melusine*. © 2018

All rights reserved, including the right to reproduce this book, or portions thereof, in any form.

The right of Storm Constantine and Andrew Collins and their contributors to be identified as the authors of this work has been asserted by them in accordance with the Copyright, Designs and Patents Act, 1988.

Cover Art: Brom
Cover Design: Danielle Lainton
Interior Layout: Storm Constantine
Interior Illustrations by Danielle Lainton, Storm Constantine and Ruby, as indicated within the book.

All other illustrations and plate pictures are from the authors' personal collections. Every attempt has been made by the authors to clarify the ownership of illustrations used in this book. Any oversights or omissions will be corrected in future editions.

Set in Book Antiqua

MB0198
ISBN: 978-1-912241-06-4

A Megalithica Books Publication
http://www.immanion-press.com
info@immanion-press.com

Contents

By Storm Constantine & Andrew Collins, except where otherwise indicated.

Archetypal Bad Girls and Femmes Fatales – Caroline Wise	7
Meetings with Dark Goddesses – Storm Constantine	11
The Garden of Gateways	15

Mistresses of Night and Stars

The Night Dwellers	29
Asteria: Seer of Stars and Darkness	31
Meeting Asteria	33
Brėkšta: Dusk Walker	39
Meeting Brėkšta	40
Nótt: Bringer of Night	45
Meeting Nott	47
Nyx: Eternal Night	53
Meeting Nyx	55
Ashina: The Grey She-Wolf – Deborah Cartwright	61
Meeting Ashina – Deborah Cartwright	67

Dark Mothers

The Fearsome Dame	77
Berchta: The White Wife	79
Meeting Berchta	82
Kali: The Beautiful, Black Devourer	87
Meeting Kali	91
Sedna: Vengeful Mother of the Sea	97
Meeting Sedna	99
Babalon: Mother of Mystery	105
Meeting Babalon	109

Goddesses of War and Battlegrounds

Fierce Sisters	117
Andraste: Goddess of the Iceni Queen	119
Meeting Andraste	122
The Morrígan: Walker of the Battlefields	127
Meeting The Morrígan	131
Pakhet: Huntress of the Red Desert	135
Meeting Pakhet	137
Scáthach: Queen of the Proving Grounds	141
Meeting Scáthach	144
Sekhmet: Eye of Ra	151
Meeting Sekhmet – Maggie Jennings	153

Goddesses of Chaos and Ecstasy

Wild Women	161
Eris: Strife, Striving and Mischief	163

Meeting Eris	167
Aphrodite: Mistress of Wild Desire	173
Meeting Aphrodite	177
Erzuli Danto: Mother of Freedom – Richard Ward	183
Meeting Erzuli Danto – Richard Ward	186
Tiamat: Primordial Chaos	191
Meeting Tiamat	194

Tricksters and Crones

Bogey Women	201
Baba Yaga: Witch of the Wood	203
Meeting Baba Yaga	205
Black Annis: Child Stealer of the Hills	211
Meeting Black Annis – Caroline Wise	214
The Cailleach: Witch of Harsh Winter	219
Meeting the Cailleach	222
Hecate: Mistress of the Crossroads	227
Meeting Hecate (with Caroline Wise)	231

Women as Demons

The Non-Conformists	239
Lilith: Heroine of Emancipation	241
Meeting Lilith	244
Lamia: Beautiful Serpent	249
Meeting Lamia	252
Melusine: Shape-Shifting Fairy	257
Meeting Melusine – Caroline Wise	261
Agrat Bat Mahlat: Daughter of Lilith	267
Meeting Agrat Bat Mahlat	269

Queens of Death

Of Graveyards and Underworlds	275
Akhlys: The Mist of Death	277
Meeting Akhlys	279
Dea Tacita: She of the Silence	285
Meeting Dea Tacita	288
Ereshkigal: Queen of Irkalla	293
Meeting Ereshkigal	297
Hel: Queen of the Dead	303
Meeting Hel – Caroline Wise	306
Nephthys: Lady of Light and Darkness	311
Meeting Nephthys – Maggie Jennings	314

Embarking upon Further Journeys	318
About the Contributors	319

Archetypal Bad Girls and Femmes Fatales

Caroline Wise

Many of the goddesses from the ancient world, and also those in living traditions and religions, are often acknowledged in contemporary neo-paganism as being 'dark' or having dark aspects. This concept is new; they wouldn't have been seen as such in the ancient world, whose poets revealed complex characters. These goddesses derive from harsh times, when childbirth frequently killed, when famine could come in an instant, from storms or plagues of locusts, and wipe out your kin. Times when invasions were often on the horizon, and when tempests or calms could bring death at sea. In the distant past, humans attempted to strike deals with their deities, and made offerings to them, as well as pleas for survival, including fending off the hungry wolf stalking their livestock.

The Cailleach of Winter came inexorably, whether people liked it or not, as did night and disaster. These darker aspects of the goddess were still acknowledged as much as the goddesses of light and plenty and even they sometimes had a dual nature.

The dark goddesses include vengeful goddesses, war goddesses, jealous goddesses, and tricksters. In legend, for example, solar Sekhmet tries to destroy humanity for not showing enough respect to the Sun God. But she was also venerated as a mother and a healer of bones. Ishtar is a goddess of war but also of love. We think of Aphrodite as a lovely goddess, but love can bring the cruellest pain, and Aphrodite can laugh at the love-lorn. Sirens would drag sailors down to a watery grave. Life was short, and the death goddesses had an important function and place in the circle of living and the passage of the soul. What we see in our own time as 'dark' was no less frightening in the past, but people clothed the various forces in the masks of those aspects and did not dress them up as cosy companions. They had a role.

Such archetypal bad girls are echoed in the *femme fatales* of stories ancient and modern, and in the scary figures of local folklore. I have noticed two issues with the modern idea of dark goddesses: some now claim that they're not really dark but sweetness and light and have merely been given a bad spin by Christianity, or alternatively that they are power-givers to contemporary women. When studying these goddesses, I found it clear this is not the whole story, which is more nuanced. Claiming they've been misrepresented by Christianity often does them a disservice, turning them into something they are not, seeking to clip their power. The second reimagining is more positive, as long as we remember that we do not serve the Goddess or the world by being combative warriors and vengeful all the time, but only when an injustice or cause demands it!

The goddesses are multifaceted, in the same way most humans are. We are not always nice: we can be kind, thoughtful, greedy, or spiteful, depending on all kinds of variables. Some may love us and some fear us, depending on which aspect we reveal to them in any situation. The goddesses can certainly be seen as representatives of aspects of human nature, and also as preternatural beings with the wisdom to rise above it, able to intervene in the problems of humans, if the right call signs are made.

The dark goddesses can be guardians of the wildwood groves and crazed mountain-top revels, of the unseen world of spirits, of the cosmos, but also mundane reality, where they were invoked, celebrated, and petitioned.

Storm Constantine and Andrew Collins have chosen a wide and fascinating group of goddesses for this book, including some who are not so well-known. The pathworkings to meet these entities, and explore their realms through meditation and intuition, will help you gain insight into these oft misunderstood deities. May they cast aside their dark hooded cloaks and reveal not the clichéd beautiful maiden, but rather the wisdom teacher within.

Dark Goddess by Danielle Lainton

Meetings with Dark Goddesses

Storm Constantine

We fear the dark, yet we crave it. We get frightened, and yet fear is frequently experienced (and described) as delicious.

The dark goddess is set apart from the usual pagan trinity of maiden, mother and crone, although she is often seen in one of those forms. Other goddesses personify female traits, such as the benevolent mother, the innocent maiden, the whore (or rather the knowing, sexually-active female), or the wise hag. There are also benign goddesses of natural forces, such as the sea, the stars, the moon. While, in legend, female deities might sometimes have been vengeful if crossed, they were also, in a way, comforting, because they were - and are - recognisable. But is not the feminine essentially mysterious and full of secrets - beyond recognition?

The dark goddess is unsettlingly different from the common conceptions of *acceptable* womanhood. She is fearsome, lustful, unpredictable, dispassionate, cruel, often deadly. She is Mother Nature without mercy. She is the Ice Maiden with no heart. She is the bloody scavenger of the battlefields. She is the huntress of the Moon. She is the monster of the *vagina dentata*, who may tear a man's masculinity from him when he is most vulnerable. She is the insanity of obsessive desire. She is the queen of the dead, and the avatar of madness. She manifests too in handmaidens of male gods, such as in the bacchantes and maenads - women who think nothing of hunting and devouring their fellow humans, primarily men.

As a symbol of nature, the goddess must necessarily be brutal and impartial. While her fecundity ensures human survival, the withdrawal of her favours is a death sentence.

Some modern pagans choose to endow the goddess with kind and motherly qualities, to see her entirely as a benign nurturer, full of love for creation. Earlier peoples were more attuned to her actual nature, since they had to live in it. Modern humans are divorced from the realities of making fire, hunting and gathering food, and being easy prey to disease, injury and infirmity. Our 'advanced' society protects us to a large degree from these demons. But to early humans, the supernatural forces which they believed governed all living things were monsters to be appeased. They might strike out without provocation and bring disaster. It could have seemed as if they revelled in human suffering and delighted in causing it.

Women too must have been regarded as innately mysterious, being able to become pregnant and give birth. During sex, a woman might seem to have immense power – a male can be helpless in the throes of pleasure. Also, the intoxicating allure of a female, which can unravel the most austere mind into a kind of lunacy, was no doubt a component in the imagining and creation of the Dark Goddess. To a person obsessed, love is dark and uncontrollable, hungry and terrible – not simply the result of hormonal or chemical processes in the body. The beloved is the Devourer, sucking sanity and strength from their victim. In such a spirit were goddesses – or perhaps more accurately demonesses – like Lilith born.

An interesting aspect of the way the feminine in the divine is viewed nowadays is that figures from folklore, myth and ancient history who were originally mortal women – albeit extraordinary women – have in many cases now been transformed by modern pagans into goddesses. Some of them might have begun as witches and sorceresses, or Underworld queens, or demons to be feared, or alluring but deadly nymphs, or wise crones, or terrifying hags of the night. But they embody principles and states – not just of womanhood but humanity and nature in general. They are symbols. Paganism isn't so much about worshipping gods and goddesses but respecting these powerful archetypes and working with what they symbolise to effect change – whether in the self or in reality.

This book is not academic, nor can we say that a great deal of it is historical fact. Myths and legends spring from oral traditions, and even in the ancient world, different writers put their own interpretation on a story, made it fit another tale they were writing, or simply made up something new that was exciting and added to the original. Folk tales and legends could also be used in connection with political propaganda, such as seems to have happened with the stories of the Celtic queen Boudicca and Andraste – the goddess she allegedly worshipped.

In compiling this book, we've examined a lot of sources and pulled from them those elements that fit comfortably together and stuck to the themes with which we were working. Some of the information we discovered, while plainly recently-invented, felt like a good fit to the original myth – somehow *authentic* (certainly for us) – so we've included small details from such sources that enhance the stories. Other sources we looked at, which were devoted to modern paganism, gave versions of the stories that were plainly little to do with the original goddess and involved some wishful thinking, which we felt took that goddess away from what she symbolises. These, to us, didn't feel authentic. Our preference is to remain true to the symbol, the raw inner truth of what a goddess meant to people in the past and what she can mean to us now. But that said, if someone else wants to turn a bloodthirsty goddess of war into a nurturing mother goddess, and it works for them, that's fine – *for them*. We can each have our own interpretations of these ancient symbols.

There is no 'true' story for any of the women, goddesses and demons in this book. Even if the original narratives spoken around a fire had a grain of truth in them, perhaps based upon distant memories of people who once actually lived and loved and warred, then they were embellished with layers of story-telling. An old woman who lives alone, and is a little eccentric, becomes a wicked, child-stealing witch in the mind of a story-teller, because that story is so much more exciting and chilling than the sad truth of a perhaps sick old woman living a lonely life and being ostracised. Quite often, such stories were told to keep children in line. 'Behave or the witch will get you!'

None of the 'original' stories were newspaper reports that were filmed or photographed. They were fictions that have been added to continually. There was no verifiable account of what the goddess Hera did to the women her husband Zeus repeatedly seduced. There were no witnesses to the scenes when murders took place or spells were cast. There was no newspaper headline 'Sexy Lilith walks out on distraught hubby Adam, takes up with demon hunk'. Why? – because they were always make-believe, and the tales grew and changed over the centuries, if not millennia in some cases. But still the germ, the seed remains.

Goddesses of every hue are illustrations of our deepest desires, fears, ideals, hopes and expectations. They are the elaborate masks we place upon the formless energy of the universe, the forces of which it is comprised. We shape their essence to our own purposes and intentions.

When we work with the energy of these powerful entities we learn more about ourselves and how to control our lives. Within their stories lie truths about the human condition. The shadowy beings you'll find within these pages can help with liberation from conditioning and fear and may even bestow the wisdom of the ages.

The Garden of Gateways

This book explores a diverse selection of goddesses or female supernatural beings, found in different cultures. In order to interact with these entities, you'll be visiting a visualised garden, which provides portals to different etheric realms, but for each pathworking you'll begin at the same spot – the centre of the garden.

You should imagine this garden as the archetype of a perfect landscape that has been subtly designed to look natural. It has four directions, each of which represents one of the four elements of air, fire, water and earth. The fifth element, spirit, is represented by the centre of the garden where the visualisations always begin.

Within the pathworkings, you'll be working with the Western Tradition correspondences of the elements and the directions. In this system, the east corresponds to air, the south to fire, the west to water and the north to earth. These correspondences also resemble a clock face representing times of day and the seasons of the year:

Air: Dawn, Spring
Fire: Noon, Summer
West: Twilight, Autumn
North: Midnight, Winter

These correspondences are used as maps to the deities and entities encountered in the visualisations. They have a specific meaning and purpose in this work to guide you to particular landscapes and entities. In their capacity of relating to the season, they might also dictate how the environment of an entity is visualised. The majority of hag goddesses and spirits are associated with winter, for example, so their direction is generally the north. Goddesses associated with the element of water will be approached from the west, as would entities associated with the early evening, the setting sun and the rising of the moon.

Before you start the goddess pathworkings themselves, we advise you to visit the garden in visualisation and become familiar with its layout.

You may explore all the areas of the garden in one visualised visit, or if you prefer, you could split this up into four visits, and spend more time in each area, absorbing and imagining their appearance and pathways. This is entirely up to the individual and how much information you feel you can absorb in one meditation.

You can also repeat the visualisations several times in order to become thoroughly familiar with them.

It's important that the garden and the environments beyond it are entirely yours – we won't go into absolute, minute detail about what each area looks like. We'll provide the basic imagery, but you should make these places your own, your private temple and sacred space. The paths of the garden lead you out to specific points that may be different each time.

Remember always to make notes of every visit to the Garden of Gateways. Memories can fade fast, and it's helpful to record your experiences for later reference.

Visiting the Garden

Choose a room, or an outdoors location, where you won't be disturbed while you meditate. If you wish, you can play music that feels appropriate to you, or even recordings of natural sounds, such as rainfall or birdsong.

If you'll be meditating in the evening, you can aid concentration by turning down the lights, and perhaps lighting a candle. Have this flickering beside you. You can also play some appropriate music and burn some incense. These preparations will help create the correct state of mind.

Compose yourself for meditation by breathing deeply for a couple of minutes, allowing the everyday world and its concerns to float away from your mind. You may either sit or lie down. Allow your body to relax.

Now imagine that the everyday world is fading away into a soft mist. The mist is neither warm nor cold, but simply comfortable. Continue to breathe deeply as you visualise this.

Gradually, the mist begins to melt away and a new landscape is revealed to you. Allow the time of day to come naturally to you – it might be dark or light.

You find yourself standing upon a lawn surrounded by tall hedges. There are gaps in the hedges at each point of the compass, like a gateway. At present, you can't make anything out beyond the hedge itself, but you know instinctively you are facing north.

In the middle of the lawn is an old, gnarled apple tree, marking the heart of the garden, its omphalos, or centre of power. Its bark might be grey, and its ancient limbs bent, but it still flourishes abundantly. Depending on what time of year it is, the tree will be thick with green leaves, and in the appropriate season blossom or fruit. In addition, below it is a spring, from a deep source in the ground.

If you ever feel you've lost your way in a pathworking, remember that your main spiritual self remains in the garden always, so you can never truly be lost. This is your place of connection between the worlds. Some part of you will always remain there to draw back your spirit essence to this spot.

The North

Begin your explorations in the northern area of the garden. As you are already facing north, go towards the gap in the hedge directly ahead of you. You emerge into the garden itself, into an area that's designed to look like woodland. This is the area of the element of earth.

As you walk the night comes down and soon you find your way in darkness. The garden here is clearly a winter landscape. The trees are almost bare, and it might be snow-covered. But the sky above is clear and bright, a tapestry of stars to guide your way.

You come eventually to the mouth of a cave, a natural symbol of what the ancients referred to either as the Beneath World or the Underworld. This pathway provides access to a perceived otherworld, a realm usually reached only during dreams and shifted states of consciousness. It also offers a route of access to the stars, and the turning point of the heavens, around which the starry canopy revolves.

When you step into the cave, with the intention of meeting a particular goddess, the path beyond the entrance will change to the appropriate access point.

For now, you're not here to meet a goddess, simply to familiarise yourself with the lay of the land.

You enter the cave and find yourself in a small chamber, with a narrow doorway opposite. Go to this natural passageway and follow it. A dim glow illuminates your way, but you cannot tell where this light is coming from. There may be twists and turns in the path, perhaps the suggestion of other passages leading off to left or right, but you keep to the main path. Be aware that when you return to this cave in the future, with a particular location in mind, you'll have to be focused, so that the twists and turns of the path don't confuse you.

The passageway eventually emerges into the open air. You find yourself in a new environment, high above a mountainous landscape. You stand upon a precipice and overhead the night sky is thickly jewelled with stars. You feel as if you could run off the edge of the precipice and launch yourself upwards, into space. Approaching the edge, you look over and see beneath what seems to be a bottomless canyon. In the sky ahead of you shines the heavenly lantern of the bright northern star. To reach the stars from this point you would have to leap into the sky.

Now think about how the cave and its passages can take you to other places, different chambers, different landscapes and worlds. Be aware that the cave entrance you first came across is a portal to more than one location. If you have clear intent of mind, you can go wherever you wish and encounter the particular goddess you desire to meet.

Stand for some minutes at this spot and be aware of the properties of this direction. If you wish to, you can take on the form of a bear or a snow leopard, or another animal associated with winter or darkness, and explore the environment.

Then, when you are ready to return, retrace your steps to the centre of the garden.

The East

You'll next explore the eastern area, which is the realm of the element of air.

In the centre of the garden, face the east. Walk to the gap in the hedge in that direction and pass through it.

Beyond the hedge, you find a straight path in a formal garden, which leads to a high fence and a gate. The time is early morning, and birds sing to greet the dawn.

As you follow the path, you notice that the season is spring time and early flowers are blooming. Leaves are unfurling their leaves and young animals can be glimpsed between the foliage of shrubs.

Follow the path and when you reach the gate, open it and pass through.

Beyond, you find that the path continues, now widening into a track. The sun is rising at the horizon and the path seems to lead right to it. This is the realm of the element of air. To left and right are mountains and hills, a feeling of space and airiness. The air feels crystal clear, invigorating to breathe.

The realm of air is filled with winds. The mountains are high and sharp, and buildings upon them will be adorned with wind chimes and other items that play with the element of air. Think about objects that are affected by air – the crack of pennants and flags, or elaborate kites anchored by strings to the earth in the shape of mythical creatures, or hot air balloons with ornate patterns on them. There might be windmills of strange design, or land vehicles powered by the wind having sails, or gliders in the sky. Soaring birds ride the thermals. The only limit is your imagination.

You follow the path to the east for about a hundred yards and eventually come to a crossroads. It might be that sometimes you will head off to left or right, but the main purpose of this path is to lead you forward to your future: it is the Path of Destiny. It signifies the new dawn, the beginning of what is to come.

Stand for some minutes at this spot and be aware of the properties of this direction. Become a bird if you so desire and explore the environment. Then retrace your steps to the centre of the garden.

The South

Now it's time to explore south of the garden, the realm of the element of fire.

In the centre of the garden, face the south. Walk to the gap in the hedge in that direction and pass through it.

You find yourself in an area of the garden reminiscent of hot climates, planted with succulents and desert trees. It is clearly summer time. The path leads straight to the south but on either side are formal gardens of palms and the voluptuous flowers associated with the warmer lands. The air is full of their intoxicating perfume.

As in the east, you walk towards a high fence, in which there is a wooden gate.

When you open the gate and step through you're aware immediately of great heat, but this does not hurt or harm you. If clouds are in the sky, they are limned with the radiance of the sun's rays.

The path ahead of you leads to where the noonday sun hangs high in the sky, blazing on a hot summer's day.

On one side of you is what seems to be a desert, stretching far away into a haze, while on the other side are burned fields. The desert is not devoid of life, but full of it. There are mountainous areas, and plant life that thrives in dry conditions. There are wadis and oases where rare and precious water is found. Above you, you're aware of wide-winged birds, carrion eaters, circling over landscape. You can hear their cries. Other animals of the desert, such as lions, coyotes and hyenas prowl among the dry rocks. There might be ancient ruins here, guarding the secrets of vanished races.

On the other side of the path lies the cremation ground, the burning fields. This might be a place of the dead, where human remains are burned upon sacred pyres, or exposed on tall wooden frames for scavengers like vultures, crows and ravens to consume. Or it might be fields stretching away to far, sun-scorched hills. In the fields, the first crops have been cut and the stubble will soon be burnt. Unlit bonfires might wait here to be ignited.

Be aware that the landscape might change whenever you pass through the gate. You might emerge into a full desert or else a cremation ground. You might find yourself in ruins beneath a scorching sun.

Stand for some minutes at this spot and be aware of the properties of this direction. Become a desert creature, or even a jackal of the cremation grounds, and explore the environment if you wish to. Then return to the centre of the garden.

The West

The final direction you'll explore is the west, which is the realm of the element of water.

In the centre of the garden, face the west and walk to the gap in the hedge and pass through it.

You find a rising pathway before you, set between ornamental rockeries. Trees are dressed in autumn's finery; reds, oranges and gold. The air smells of smoke and fruit.

The path turns into steps and high walls of rock covered in ivy and other greenery surround you on either side of the path. Now you can hear the sound of rushing water.

You pass through a stone portal and find yourself beside a pool. Water gushes into it from a small, yet powerful waterfall. You're aware that this is an ancient power site that people have augmented over the years to form an ornate water garden of tiers and pools and waterfalls.

The pool before you is semi-circular and its surface bubbles from the waters of the fall. You're aware that you could use this pool for scrying, by gazing into the waters. You know that you'll be able to make contact with certain goddesses here, because you can access various watery domains from this site.

The pool is around fifteen to twenty feet across and now you notice that on the right side of it, a stream flows away beneath a curtain of ivy. You lift the ivy aside and see that the water pours down, out of sight, over a series of steps cut into the rock. Moisture also trickles down the mossy and lichened rock walls to either side of the narrow steps.

Begin to walk down the steps. Perhaps you are barefoot, and the refreshing, cold water flows over your feet. The steps turn corners to left and right, and as they do so the water becomes deeper and flows more fiercely. You realise it would now be impossible to turn back and climb up the steps.

You lose your footing, because the steps have in fact disappeared. You're now in a natural, rocky chute, down which you travel with the tumbling waters. This doesn't feel dangerous or frightening, simply exhilarating.

After a short time, the chute levels out and the flow of the water becomes calmer once more. You are moving towards the ocean. Soon, you emerge upon the shore, and here you get to your feet. Shallow, fresh water still flows around you. You find you're in a cove with a wide sandy beach. Ahead of the you is the sea and the stream you followed flows into it.

Evening is beginning to fall, and the sky to the west is reddened by the sinking sun. Any clouds in the sky are illumined by these crimson rays.

The cove is surrounded on three sides by high, white cliffs. For some minutes absorb the ambience of the landscape. Be aware that you may call upon goddesses of the sea in this place, but also that the water garden far above may lead you to other environments, different goddesses.

Spend some time absorbing the ambience of this location, focusing upon the aspect of water, and of twilight and the setting sun. This too, as much as the cave in the north, might lead to the otherworld, the realm of spirits, since the west in many cultures is identified with the point of access to the land of the dead. This is very often reached via a journey along the Milky Way in its role as the Path of Souls.

When you're ready, return to the centre of the garden. Once your exploration of the garden is complete, and you're fully familiar with its paths and directions, you may move on to pathworkings with the goddesses.

Performing the Pathworkings

There are, of course, other ways to conduct the visualisation exercises in this book, which do not involve closing your eyes and entering a meditational state of consciousness. If you're unused to visualising, you might find it easier to use the text itself to focus on the realms of the Dark Goddess. The style in which we wrote the book facilitates this approach. In which case, simply imagine yourself in the garden, heading off in the direction indicated, then simply read slowly through the selected pathworking. Use its words to guide you as you enter a virtual 'daydream', in which you can feel and sense yourself in the presence of the goddess in question. For this, all you need is a quiet environment and a generally peaceful state of mind, free from the usual pressures of the day.

If you want to, you can take breaks from the reading to examine the thoughts and feelings your inner journey might've raised in your mind, or to explore a path your imagination has revealed to you. Once your creative mind has free rein, the visualisation can almost take on a life of its own. Flow with this. See where it leads.

Visualisation is like a muscle. If you exercise it, it becomes more supple. The more times you perform the pathworkings in this book, the more you'll feel immersed in them and perhaps desire to explore their landscapes further, meeting with whatever entities might reside there.

Reading doesn't have to be simply a case of looking at words printed on a page. It can create a kind of virtual reality in your mind. For example, when you're reading a novel, this phenomenon helps immerse you entirely in a fictional world. For a while, it's as if you really are *in* that imagined environment. Reading can quite literally take the mind into a light, shifted state of consciousness, from which you can return to the waking world at any time. Performing the pathworkings this way might also allow you to ponder more easily the nature of the goddesses you meet, as well as their meaning to you, to their followers, and to humankind as a whole.

Some idea of the power of words comes from the folklore traditions of the Isle of Man. It was said that simply by reciting stories of fairies a person could become enchanted, and in doing so enter their realm of existence. It was for this reason that the reading of fairy stories became outlawed, lest innocent people be drawn into the devilish world of these supernatural creatures. Nothing like this is going to happen to readers of this book, of course, although it *is* hoped the words we've carefully woven will permit a closer connection with the liminal realms within which preter-human intelligences might dwell.

Mistresses of Night
and Stars

Adapted from a vintage illustration

The Night Dwellers

To ancient peoples the sky was the realm of gods. How far away was it? All those bright points of light that seemed to move around the heavens – what were they? The stars themselves might have been seen as spirits, incomprehensible beings watching over the earth. And, to the Romans, the brightest lights of all represented the gods – Mars, Jupiter, Mercury, Saturn and Venus. The skies were mysterious. When the sun slunk into the shadows at the end of day, its mysteries were partly revealed.

The goddesses in this section were chosen for their affinity to the night, to dusk or to stars. The Greek stellar goddess Asteria is associated with divination by night and the stars. Lithuanian Brėkšta is a goddess so old that very little is known about her, but she was said to walk the twilight between night and day. In Norse mythology, Nótt pulled the darkness across the heavens, bringing night to the earth. And the Greek Nyx is night personified, giving birth to dreams but also to light and day.

When exploring the goddesses and female spirits of the aspects of darkness, where best to begin but with night itself? We can imagine ourselves back in ancient times, seeing the firmament as our ancestors might have done, creating explanations for the wonders we see above us in the dark; the unfathomable realm where the night goddesses were born. They were shaped from fear, from wonder, from curiosity – and the desire *to know*. Some believe the future is written in the sky, and the stars are the script that form it. In dreams and visions are fates predicted. In darkness.

Asteria by Danielle Lainton

Asteria
Seer of Stars and Darkness

*Neither by ship nor on foot
would you find the marvellous road
to the assembly of the Hyperboreans.*

*Never the Muse is absent
from their ways: lyres clash and flutes cry,
and everywhere maiden choruses whirling.
Neither disease nor bitter old age is mixed
in their sacred blood; far from labour and battle they live.*

Pindar, Greek Poet

Within Greek mythology there are nearly a dozen women, goddesses or spirits with the name Asteria, but most importantly she was a goddess associated with the stars. Her name meant 'of the stars' 'or starry one', and she was particularly associated with falling stars.

She is not to be confused with a deity of similar name, Astraea, who was a virgin goddess of innocence and purity. While Astraea's name is also associated with the stars, (meaning 'star maiden), she was the daughter of Astraeus and Eos. Astraeus was a Titan, god of the dusk, while Eos, a Titaness, personified the dawn. Their daughter Astraea became connected with the concept of justice, rather than stars and the night.

Asteria, on the other hand, is entirely associated with the stars and was also a Titaness – part of the lineage of giant deities that began with Ouranos, or Uranus, (the heavens) and Gaia (the earth). She was the daughter of Coeus, a god of the intellect and/or the enquiring mind, and

Phoebe, a goddess of the moon, whose name meant 'shining'. Phoebe was associated with oracles and prophecy. Asteria had a sister, Leto, who became the mother of Artemis and Apollo, after attracting the lustful attentions of the god Zeus – not an uncommon hazard for females in Greek mythology.

According to the ancient legends, Asteria too ignited the lust of Zeus. After the Fall of the Titans, when the gods of Olympus warred with the giants and won, Zeus pursued Asteria across the heavens. She managed to escape his unwanted advances by transforming herself into a quail and throwing herself into the ocean. Here, she became the island of Delos. Later, her sister Leto gave birth to the god Apollo upon this island. The pregnant Leto had incurred the wrathful jealousy of Hera, Zeus's consort, who decreed that every land should shun her rival and expel her. Delos, however, was unattached to the ocean floor, so wasn't technically land. Here, Leto found sanctuary upon the body of her sister.

There is some association, albeit tenuous, between Asteria, her sister Leto and her nephew Apollo, and the mythical northern land of Hyperborea. This land was said to be populated by giants – perhaps Titans – and Apollo was venerated by them. They were believed to have visited Delos because of this connection. Leto, in some traditions, was said to have been born in Hyperborea, which in its original form was identified with the Altai Mountains of southern Siberia and Mongolia.

Strong imagery concerning the far north came to us as we were working on the visualisations for this book, so we've chosen to emphasise this connection.

As well as being a star goddess, Asteria was also associated with divination, in the same way her mother was. It's believed she presided over 'nocturnal divination', practices conducted only by night. This would include oneiromancy, or divination by dreams, as well as astrology, which is of course divination by the stars. Therefore, she's an appropriate goddess to call upon for prophetic dreamwork or the interpretation of dreams. The falling stars with which she's connected could also denote prophecies.

Asteria had one daughter with a distant cousin, Perses, who was a god associated with destruction. That daughter was Hecate, who was said to have been honoured by Zeus above all others – Hecate, the dark mistress of witchcraft, who you will meet later in this book.

Meeting Asteria

Begin the pathworking by entering the Garden of Gateways. To meet with Asteria, you will go into the northern part of the garden.

Find your way to the cave in the north of the garden. You pass through the passageways in this place easily, since on this occasion your road is straight. You are seeking the stars on the other side of the cave complex.

You emerge onto the precipice beyond the cave, where you can see the night sky. The stars revolve around their turning point in the heavens. The heavens seem to turn like a Ferris wheel. The stars rise up from the northeast, pass the North Star, then set in the northwest of the sky. Some stars don't even set. These are circumpolar stars, which means they never vanish beneath the horizon, since they are close to the celestial pole. These stars were of particular interest to scholars in ancient times, because they were believed to have the power to vanquish death.

At the edge of precipice, you hold out your arms and leap up into the air, knowing instinctively you will not fall. You will fly.
Once in the air, project yourself towards the north. The light of the stars illuminates the celestial path. Among the constellations, your attention is drawn to Deneb, the bright star of Cygnus, the swan, which you know is associated with Asteria. This star blazes at the turning point of the heavens, its place in the sky easily found since it stands where the Milky Way, the bright stream of stars forming the edge of our galaxy, is seen to fork into two separate arms.
Glancing down, you find you're flying over a landscape. It's so far below, you can barely make out the hills, forests, valleys, settlements and roads beneath you. Gradually you swoop down and as you draw closer to the ground, you see a large lake below you, illuminated by cold, clear starlight. You sense you are in the extreme north, and at a time far back in history, in the ancient land known as Hyperborea, the home of a race of giants. You finish your descent and land lightly upon the shore of the lake.
Now, you see that there's a small island in the centre of the lake, which you're aware is the original Delos, also known as the White Island. You can see a round Classical style temple there, which is roofless, open to the sky. The temple's round shape represents a reflection of the cup of the heavens.

You notice a white boat floats upon the water nearby, and you sense it's waiting to provide you with passage to the island.
Once you step into the boat, it begins to glide over the water, swiftly and effortlessly. In just a few moments, you

are stepping out of it onto the shore of the island. You walk towards the temple.

When you reach this building, you pass between the columns to its centre. Here, there is a raised dais and burning upon it is a white fire; it is unnaturally white, the flame of a star.

You become aware of another presence besides yourself, and now see the goddess Asteria standing upon the dais, illuminated by the white starfire. She's immensely tall, a giantess. You think about how myths and legends are created, and that perhaps this woman is the memory of a race that once lived upon the earth, an earlier form of humankind, a hybrid of more than one proto-human population.

Asteria wears a midnight blue robe, in the style of Ancient Greece. She has platinum white hair, which is pinned upon her head into the shape of a cone. This is to represent a white flame. It reminds you of the shape of a whelk shell. Within her hair hang tiny precious stones that glint in the starlight. Over her robe, she wears a cloak of swan feathers. The head and neck of the swan are curled around her neck, like a stole. She beckons you to her.

You step up onto the dais, and at Asteria's gesture, you gaze into the starfire. In your mind, the goddess tells you that you will be shown a prophecy in the flame. As you stare into it, you glimpse the future, or aspects of your life that require fulfilment. You also see fleeting images of the past, present and future woven together.

As you gaze into the starfire, it expands outwards to embrace you. It engulfs the goddess, even the temple itself. In this whirling radiance, which feels cool rather than hot, you see images of your past present and future all around you. Clarity will come to you now, information about the directions you can take into the future to achieve your goals in life.

Before leaving the pathworking, ask Asteria about her inner mysteries. Ask about Hyperborea itself. This is the place beyond the north wind, where Apollo would drive a chariot drawn by swans. It is the land of his mother, Leto, the place of origin of their cult.

When you are ready to conclude the pathworking, return to the garden by visualising the central tree clearly. This is your beacon and your guide. Be aware that a part of yourself remained there while you were travelling. It was and is your anchor. Return to that part of yourself simply by thinking this. You find yourself standing beneath the tree, feeling calm and refreshed. Return to normal consciousness and open your eyes.

Asteria's Island by Storm Constantine

Brėkšta by Danielle Lainton

Brėkšta
Dusk Walker

'Not all dreams are significant or worth remembering.
But the ones that are... happen again.
So, wait for the dream to return. And never be afraid. Instead,
consider it an opportunity to learn something profound and
possibly wondrous about yourself.'

From *The Perpetual Calendar of Inspiration*
by Vera Nazarian,

Brėkšta is an ancient goddess from Lithuania – so ancient in fact that much of what we know about her is speculation. Most of the existing information derives from the work of two Polish historians - Jan Łasicki, who referred to her as Breksta in the 17th century, and Theodor Narbutt who named her as Brekszta in the 19th century. Both of these renditions are 'Latinised'. Her original name has been lost, but she is now known by the properly-accented Lithuanian name of Brėkšta.

Łasicki's and Narbutt's interpretation of Brėkšta also differed. To Łasicki she was the 'Goddess of Twilight', which gave rise to the idea that she was closely associated with another ancient Lithuanian goddess, Vakarė, and was perhaps even the same goddess. Narbutt, however, referred to her as a goddess of darkness and dreams. But as so little was actually known of these prehistoric goddess-forms, there's no evidence that either of the Polish scholars' interpretations are accurate. However, as Brėkšta is now believed to possess these qualities, they have legitimately become part of her.

Brėkšti is a term in Lithuanian, meaning 'the dusk/dawn is falling', which refers to the twilight at the start and end of day, so it's not unlikely the goddess's name derives from this word.

The name of the goddess Vakarė, with whom Brėkšta has now become intertwined, derives from 'vakaras', a Lithuanian word meaning 'evening and night'. Another form of this goddess is Vakarinė, (pronounced Va-ka-**ree**-nay) allegedly an even older name for this deity. Vakarinė is the evening star, who in Lithuanian mythology prepares a bed for the sun, known as Saulė, each night. (In Lithuanian mythology, the Sun is a female deity, which is unusual, as in most cultures it's regarded as male.) Her sister Aušrinė, the morning star, wakes Saulė every morning. In Latvia, this goddess is known as Rieteklis.

As is often the case with ancient and obscure goddesses, modern practitioners have 'tuned into' Brėkšta and enlarged upon her myth. Some regard her now as a representation of 'dream walking', even 'cave dreaming', a Neanderthal deity of astral travel, a walker of the 'in between times', the veil of dusk and dawn, when it is neither dark nor light. Seen in this way, she becomes at once an entity of mystery and fascination, who not only walks the realm of twilight but gives us a connection right back to the dreamtimes of our earliest ancestors.

Meeting Brėkšta

Begin the pathworking by entering the Garden of Gateways. To meet with Brėkšta, you will go into the northern part of the garden.

Find your way to the cave in the north of the garden. It is

night-time and the sky above you is full of stars. When you reach the entrance to the cave, you have to push aside a curtain of foliage to pass through it. Beyond, you find a chamber, where lie the remains of a fire with charred animal bones around it, but no one is here.

In the light of a sputtering torch, which is fixed to the wall, you glimpse wall paintings of animals and hunters. In the flickering glow, the crude paintings seem to move, and you catch faint impressions of the hunt; the great beasts, the danger, the skill of the hunters.

You take the torch from the wall and cross the chamber into the passageway opposite. You feel as if something is drawing you forward – smells and sounds so faint you can barely perceive them. You walk for some time, always following the indistinct scent and sounds. You are led round turns in the passageway and into other chambers, which you have to pass through, but you come across no living creature.

Eventually, you emerge into a larger chamber, where a fire burns in a circle of stones upon the floor. Directly opposite you is the entrance to a deeper chamber, from which pulses a ruddy glow, of a darker red than the fire you stand beside. You sense you should not enter this second chamber but must remain where you are standing. You cannot enter that place uninvited.

You now realise the sound you have followed is a low-pitched song, which is wordless yet somehow alluring. It appears to be coming from within the second chamber, and seems to tell of far worlds, and histories you've never heard of. The scent you followed is strong now, comprised of earth mixed with the aroma of flowers, mingled with the smell of cooking meat and burning wood.

Then, in the entranceway to the second chamber, the figure of a woman appears, silhouetted against the light behind it. As you stare at her, more details become clear. You see that she wears the skin of a great bear, with its snarling muzzle draped over the crown of her head. She's very tall, and looks muscular and strong, like a warrior. She has a long face and wild red hair, which is highlighted by the flames of the fire.

You realise that the fact she's standing upon the threshold between the two chambers is somehow significant, as if she's poised at the juxtaposition of two world or realities. She stands at the point between twilight and darkness, which also represents the border between waking and dreaming.

She is Brėkšta, goddess of lucid dreams, of journeys to far and unimagined places in the depths of night.

She's fearsome, yet you're not afraid. She's used to visitors who seek her knowledge and the experiences she can give them.

You approach and stand some feet away from her. The song that drew you to her has faded, but the scents of earth still fill your nostrils. Explain to Brėkšta why you have sought her out. Tell her that you seek her guidance and wisdom. She acknowledges this request by bowing her head to you, so that it seems for a moment you face the snout of a she-bear.

Brėkšta bids you to remain still, so that she may focus her mind and her eyes upon you. You see within her eyes the depths of night, lit by stars. The song that drew you here grows louder again. You thought it might have been Brėkšta singing, but now you realise the voice isn't hers. It comes from another place, beyond the threshold of dreams.

Brėkšta bids you to enter the inner chamber, and here there are stone ledges around the edge of the room, heaped with furs. She indicates you should lie down here, and you do so.

The song entrances you, and your eyes grow heavy.

You close them and begin to drift. You're aware of a shift in your consciousness. It's not like falling asleep and dreaming, but more like day-dreaming. In your mind, Brėkšta tells you that she will take you on a soul journey. As you travel, you may ask her questions, as you might ask questions during divination. The answers she gives will be in pictures rather than words.

As if slipping into unconsciousness, but remaining conscious at the same time, you take on an astral form. New vistas reveal themselves to you. With the goddess, you visit weird and beautiful landscapes. You journey into the future and the past.

Finally, Brėkšta takes you to her own realm. You feel enfolded by its powerful primordial nature. Here, the forests are bigger than any you've ever seen or could imagine, set in a night-time landscape of snowy mountains. In this place, in its earliest days, humankind learned to dream, to travel the spirit roads, to take soul journeys. In this place, you may ask Brėkšta to reveal to you her mysteries.

When you are ready to conclude the pathworking, return to the garden by visualising the central tree clearly. This is your beacon and your guide. Be aware that a part of yourself remained there while you were travelling. It was and is your anchor. Return to that part of yourself simply by thinking this. You find yourself standing beneath the tree, feeling calm and refreshed. Return to normal consciousness and open your eyes.

From a traditional illustration of Nótt

Nótt
Bringer of Night

Swiftly walk o'er the western wave,
Spirit of Night!
Out of the misty eastern cave,
Where, all the long and lone daylight,
Thou wovest dreams of joy and fear,
Which make thee terrible and dear--
Swift be thy flight!

Wrap thy form in a mantle grey,
Star-inwrought!
Blind with thine hair the eyes of day;
Kiss her until she be wearied out,
Then wander o'er city, and sea, and land,
Touching all with thine opiate wand –
Come, long-sought!

From: *To Night*, Rupert Brooke

In Norse mythology, Nótt is a goddess of the night – she personifies the night itself in fact – and is the grandmother of Thor. Her name means simply 'night', and she's described as being 'black and swarthy'. In any complex and wide-spread mythology, it's often difficult to untangle the complicated relationships of the gods, and the Norse tradition is no exception. Tales were subject to local variations, such as those found in the Eddas, the ancient books that preserve the myths and legends of the Norse people. There are often different versions of the same story.

In a version of the *Prose Edda*, Nótt is the daughter of a giant or Jötunn called Nörvi (also known as Narfi and

Nörr, among other variants), who came from the realm of Jötunheimr. She married three times, although there's no indication as to what happened to her first two husbands, or whether she remained married to all three of them. The first two were apparently men, while the third was of the Aesir, a god. Her first husband was Naglfari, with whom she had a son called Auðr. Her second marriage was to Annar, with whom she had a daughter named Jörð, who was a personification of the earth. Her third husband was the ása (god) Dellingr and with him she had a son, Dagr, who was a god of the day.

This son personified day in the same way his mother personified night. Dagr was said to take after his father's people, for he was bright and fair. Odin gave Nótt and Dagr the task of pulling the sun across the sky – Nótt during the night, and Dagr during the day. They were given a chariot and a horse for this purpose. Nótt was given the dark horse Hrímfaxi (Frost Mane) and Dagr the pale horse Skinfaxi (Shining Mane). Nótt would ride before her son across the heavens, and foam from Hrímfaxi's bit would drip to the earth to form the morning dew.

As 'the Bringer of Night', Nótt is sometimes shown in art as riding Hrímfaxi across the night sky, while her son Dagr, 'the Bringer of Day' is depicted riding Skinfaxi across the daylit sky

In the *Poetic Edda*, there is a tale concerning the god Thor, who wanted to know what night is called throughout the nine realms of existence, in which gods, humans, elves both dark and light, dwarves and various kinds of giant resided. He asked the dwarf Alvíss to tell him. The dwarf replied that humankind refer to Nótt simply as 'night', while the gods know her as 'darkness'. The Mighty Powers call her 'the masker', the Jötunn (or Giants) call her 'Unlight', the elves (both dark and light) refer to her as 'Joy of Sleep', while the Dwarves know her as 'Dream-

Njörun', which means 'Dream Goddess'. We can see here then several aspects of Nótt.

Some practitioners now regard Nótt as a goddess associated with creativity, particularly of the written word, who can help relieve writer's block as well as inspire new works. She's said to represent knowledge, learning, and all forms of communication, and her sacred symbols include writing utensils and books, as well as the stars. These are obviously all modern additions to Nótt, but relevant to anyone interested in working with this goddess, as the adaptation and shaping of this particular deity evolves. Perhaps because of her association with the night, she has become closely connected with dreams and dream visions, the dark cauldron from which creative ideas spring forth. When making offerings to the goddess, some practitioners suggest donating a book(s) to charity or a library.

Meeting Nótt

Begin the pathworking by entering the Garden of Gateways. To meet with Nótt, you will go into the northern part of the garden, as with the previous two goddesses associated with the night and stars. The north is the direction associated with Jötunheimr.

Find your way to the cave in the north of the garden. The entrance is clear of foliage and unguarded but appears unnaturally dark – utterly lightless. You walk into the first chamber, which on this visit is quite small. By feeling with your hands along the walls, you discover a passageway leads directly from it to the north. You must follow this path. There is no light to guide you, and you feel your way along the passageway in complete darkness. But this time you only have to walk a short way before you emerge into the open air.

It is dusk, and the light is fading rapidly. You find yourself in quite a barren area, although you sense this rather than see it, because there is little light to reveal clear details of your surroundings, and even as you take in the scene the light continues to fade. The sky above is devoid of moon or stars. You can just about discern impressions of the landscape and perceive you're standing in what seems to be a stone basin, or crater. Beyond this basin, cliffs rise all around you.

You go to stand in the middle of this basin, as your instincts tell you this is the right thing to do. You're aware of the darkness engulfing you, but you are not in any danger. Still, the scene is strange. No stars appear. No moon. Nothing to provide illumination. The sky is empty, and this is unnatural and unnerving. Now, you can't even see your own hands before your face.

Presently, you become aware of a faint, etheric blue-white light that rises up from the horizon in the distant north. This band of radiance arcs over the sky from north to south, the old path of the Milky Way. It leaves behind a trail of star dust and, as it passes overhead, you can see the trail is created by the goddess Nótt, riding an ethereal horse that has a midnight blue body and a glowing white mane and tail. Both horse and rider are gigantic. The horse is Hrímfaxi, and his hooves strike the sky to send up clouds of stardust, as a horse galloping upon the earth would raise dusty dirt from the ground. Foam from his mouth drips down to the world below to create the morning dew.

As Nótt reaches the highest point of the sky, you reach out to her with your mind. You ask to commune with her. She acknowledges your request and makes a sweeping gesture with one arm. Presently, you feel yourself rising up towards her, so that you might connect with her more intimately.

Close to, she appears fierce and powerful, as does her unearthly mount. You feel intense cold pouring from the ethereal glow surrounding Hrímfaxi and his rider. The coldness represents Nótt's place of origin – the icy mountains of Jötunheimr.

Nótt doesn't invite you to ride with her, but you're able to fly at her side as she draws the night across the sky. You're held close within the ethereal glow that surrounds her.

The goddess intimates she has something to show you, and after these words have entered your mind, you see that you're holding a large, old book. Nótt gestures that you should open it, and you do. At first, the pages are blank, but as you stare at them, words and images start to emerge. You realise that these are representations of your own thoughts and ideas. The pictures and words come ever faster as you turn the pages. It's as if you're instantly writing a book, not just about your past experiences, but those which are to come.

Now you come to a page where, as you look at it, an indication of your future path materialises. But this is not a single path. It branches and splits to represent the choices before you. This book is like a diary, your personal account, your autobiography of the future. Every time you visit Nótt, you will see further glimpses of this future being written. Nótt tells you to be aware these futures are not fixed. Each time you look at the book, the pages might change, because you have the power to change your own destiny. You have free will. All the words and images within the book are but suggested future paths and possible outcomes.

Nótt tells you to turn another page, for here you will discover her inner mysteries. You'll learn of the land of Jotunheim, and where it was, both in the mythical past and in the physical world.

Eventually, you sense you've absorbed enough information for now and close the book. At once, it disappears, taken back by the goddess, as she is the keeper of the starry library of knowledge.

You bid farewell to Nótt and relinquish the link with her. At once, you find yourself back within the basin below. Nótt now disappears towards the south, and the glow in the sky vanishes.

When you are ready to conclude the pathworking, return to the garden by visualising the central tree clearly. This is your beacon and your guide. Be aware that a part of yourself remained there while you were travelling. It was and is your anchor. Return to that part of yourself simply by thinking this. You find yourself standing beneath the tree, feeling calm and refreshed. Return to normal consciousness and open your eyes.

Nótt's Sky by Storm Constantine

Nyx by Danielle Lainton

Nyx
Eternal Night

To Nyx: The Fumigation with Torches

Nyx, parent goddess, source of sweet repose,
from whom at first both Gods and men arose,
Hear, blessed Kypris, decked with starry light,
in sleep's deep silence dwelling Ebon night!
Dreams attend your dusky train,
thrilled with the lengthened gloom and fearful strain.
Goddess of phantoms and of shadowy play,
whose drowsy power divides the natural day:
Be present, Goddess, to your suppliant's prayer,
Desired by all, whom all alike revere.

Adapted from an Orphic Hymn to Nyx
(Late Hellenistic or early Roman)

Many of the gods and goddesses in the Ancient Greek pantheon were personifications of concepts or emotions, or abstract things. Nyx was the embodiment of night and she eventually became the mother of other personifications, such as Erebus (Darkness), Aether (Brightness), Thanatos (Death), Hypnos (Sleep) and Hemera (Day), among many others. As with a lot of ancient deities, there are different and often fragmentary accounts of Nyx's relatives and qualities, but enough survives to give us a vivid picture of her. The stories reveal that she stood at the very commencement of creation, and that she was a creature of rare beauty and exceptional power, of whom even the great god Zeus was wary. Night is all-powerful.

The Greek poet Hesiod wrote that Nyx resided in

Tartarus, a part of Hades, or the Underworld. She lived there with her children Hypnos and Thanatos. Hesiod also relates that Hemera, Nyx's daughter, would leave Tartarus each day, just as her mother entered it. And when Nyx left Tartarus, Hemera would return. This symbolises the cycle of light and darkness.

Another myth, mentioned by the Greek writer Homer in *The Iliad*, relates how Hypnos once performed a favour for the goddess Hera, by putting her husband Zeus to sleep. This was so that a jealous Hera could cause trouble for Heracles, Zeus's son by another woman. (Her husband was a tireless adulterer.) Zeus was so angry when he found out about this, he wanted to cast Hypnos into the sea and drown him, but Hypnos fled quickly to his mother, Nyx. Zeus decided not to pursue Hypnos, because he feared the god's mother, or rather her power. Hypnos annoyed Zeus further times after this, and always he ran to his mother for safety, and always Zeus drew back from punishing him, such was his fear of night.

While Chaos is often regarded as the first principle of Creation, in some myths this role is ascribed to Nyx. In some accounts, she didn't live in Tartarus, but in a cave, either at the very edge of the universe, or else 'beyond the ocean'. Cronus, one of the Titans, lies asleep within this cave, rendered unconscious by an alcoholic drink made of honey. Here, his sleep is restless, for as he dreams he utters prophecies. Outside the cave, the nymph Adrasteia plays on crashing cymbals and loud drums, to accompany the chanting of Nyx, thus ensuring the movement of the universe – for it dances to the sound of Nyx's voice and Adrasteia's violent percussion.

There is also another shadowy figure associated with Nyx, and this is Phanes, who was part of the unorthodox and mystical Orphic tradition, which was regarded with suspicion by followers of the more popular religious traditions in Ancient Greece. Phanes was hatched from a 'world egg', in the primordial waters, and was androgynous in nature, a 'first born' god of light, who then went on to create the universe. His name in fact means 'light-bringer'. He presides over procreation and the generation of new life. According to one myth about him, Nyx became his wife, and he gave birth to day, as she gave birth to night. Nyx called her consort 'Protogenus'. Phanes was ruler of all the gods, but eventually passed this role to Nyx. She passed the 'sceptre' to Ouranos, who passed it to Chronos, and ultimately it passed to Zeus, who didn't let it go.

There are a host of symbols and ideas associated with Nyx. She is night, who gives birth to sleep, dreams, and death, but also to light and day. She is a creator deity and is also responsible for ensuring the continuance of the universe. She chains time in drunken sleep in her hidden cave. She is married to a divine androgyne, who's the first of all the gods and who passes rulership to her. There is a wealth of intriguing imagery and ideas connected with her.

Meeting Nyx

Begin the pathworking by entering the Garden of Gateways. To meet with Nyx, you will go into the northern part of the garden, as with the previous goddesses associated with the night and stars.

Find your way to the cave in the north of the garden. The territory is familiar to you now and you walk with confidence through the winding passageways that lead to the precipice on the other side of the cave complex.

When you emerge, dusk is falling, but you can see that below the precipice lies a rich and fertile land. You leap into the sky and fly across the landscape. Below you is a vast plain flanked by softly-rounded hills. You head towards the hills, drawn to a particular point. There are trees upon the hillsides, but these are not dense forests, more like copses and groves.

You land at the base of one of the hills and find yourself at the entrance to a large cave. The twilight is gentle and balmy, the air full of the scents of the land – flowers and honey. Above you, stars begin to appear in the sky, white and vibrant. The cave entrance is surrounded by a sea of white poppies that glow in the dim light. These plants are opiates and symbolise Nyx's power over sleep and dreaming, as well as her sons Hypnos and Somnus.

You're drawn to enter the cave, but once you cross the threshold you're faced by a diaphanous muslin curtain that hangs between you and the chamber beyond, which you can perceive is illuminated by an ethereal blue-white light. You pull the veil to one side, so that you can see beyond it. The chamber before you has been adorned and shaped. The walls are smooth and plastered, yet covered with dried poppies and their seed pods, which have been hung there. They release a soporific scent. Ornate brass lamps hang from the ceiling, in which scented oil burns, adding to the sweet aromas in the room. The ceiling is still of rough stone. The floor beneath your feet is covered in rushes that provide crude matting. You can hear the faint music of a lyre, but you can't tell where it's coming from as there is no other exit to this chamber.

In the middle of the room is what appears to be a bed fashioned of stone. It is strewn with furs and embroidered coverlets. You instincts advise you to lie down upon this bed. Despite being made of stone, the bed is surprisingly comfortable, and you feel compelled to wrap yourself in the covers and furs, which smell faintly musty but also of incense. You feel comfortably drowsy, and completely relaxed, as if you're drifting into a deep sleep.

Gradually, you become aware of presences around you and open your eyes. The lamps are dimmer now, but you catch glimpses of spirits of the night around you, flitting across the cave like dragon flies. Some remind you of fairies, while others are hideous creatures; these beings are the stuff of dreams and nightmares. Suddenly, all these creatures vanish and there is a moment of stillness.

Then you see a column of light has appeared against the wall across from you. As you stare at it you realise it's actually materialising through the wall itself. As the light approaches, you perceive a female figure within it. You realise this is Nyx, for you are within her domain. She's dressed in a long black robe, and her face is hidden by a black veil, which is sewn with myriad jewels to resemble stars. You find it slightly unnerving that you can't see her eyes or judge her expression. She stands motionless at the foot of the bed and you become aware she's connecting with your mind. This connection will allow you to dream more deeply and lucidly than you have ever done or thought possible. This is not the soul journeying of Brėkšta, but the true dreams of deep, restful sleep.

As you pass into the dream world you remain aware you're asleep. Nyx is with you and leads you through her realm and the stories associated with her. You dream of her past, the many forms she has taken in different belief systems. You catch glimpses of faraway places connected with her, and also your own life and where you might go in the future. You sense where your destiny is taking you, what part of the world, or country, what path and roads you will take to reach your goals.

Nyx tells you to clear your mind, allow yourself to dream freely, without any kind of conscious visualisation.

In this state, information will come to you. You might even fall asleep.

Eventually, you know it is time to emerge from the dreaming. You open your eyes and find yourself back in Nyx's bed. She's still there at the foot of it, but now slowly receding, drawing away from you, just as the night recedes at the break of dawn. Her influence draws back into the darkness of the north, the direction from which she came.

Then, suddenly, you realise that you're still standing on the precipice, looking towards the hill cave you've just been to in your mind.

When you are ready to conclude the pathworking, return to the garden by visualising the central tree clearly. This is your beacon and your guide. Be aware that a part of yourself remained there while you were travelling. It was and is your anchor. Return to that part of yourself simply by thinking this. You find yourself standing beneath the tree, feeling calm and refreshed. Return to normal consciousness and open your eyes.

The Cave of Nyx by Storm Constantine

Eyes of Ashina by Storm Constantine

Ashina
The Grey She-Wolf

Deborah Cartwright

> *Follow my footsteps cried the wolf,*
> *The time has come for you to join me in the Skyland...*
> *Then she left the earth climbing higher*
> *and each place she stepped the sky filled with stars.*
> *'Shun manitu tu tan ka,' we call the spirit wolves.*
> *When they climb the mountain to lift their heads and sing.*
> *Sing toward the road of stars,*
> *their songs grow stronger as their voices join.*
>
> (Siberian shamanic chant)

In the heart of Siberia lies a vast and mystical inland sea named Lake Baikul. It is home to one of the oldest human cultures – that of M'alta, which dates back 24,000 years. Some believe this important site is the true cauldron of creation for civilisation. Myths and legends abound and one of these involves the Grey She-Wolf, Ashina. Her legends, however, are widely found, from Turkey, across Siberia to the Russian-Asian border of the Ural Mountains, to China and across the Eurasian Steppes.

To the shamanic cultures of prehistoric times – and on into the present day – Ashina was the Keeper of Fertility and of Earth Water. Earth water, distinctly different from the water of rain or melted snow, refers to rivers, lakes and underground mountain streams: the water that provides sustenance for communities. A clan formed around Lake Baikal that came to be known as the Ashina – the clan of the Grey She-Wolf.

Strictly speaking, Ashina is not a goddess but more a powerful spirit of the land, as well as a living being from whom the Clan of Ashina believe they are physically descended. Prehistoric tribes of Siberia possessed sophisticated forms of art and tool technology. Recent evidence suggests that they domesticated wolves, rode horses and understood the movement of the heavens and celestial bodies.

These tribes were a shamanic culture who practised a form of what is called animism. The primary understanding of animism is that all things have a spirit or energetic life force that connects everything together as one consciousness. Through this unity of spirit force, it is possible for a singular mind to communicate and connect to the minds of other beings, animals and organic things. Shamans of an animistic culture believe they can communicate with the spirits of all living things, such as trees, rivers and of course animals. Indeed, animistic shamans claim to be able to become animals, or shapeshift into animal forms, by using and manipulating the animistic life force omnipresent upon the living planet and the other worlds beyond it.

The soul or spirit of a living being is the central focus of animistic shamanism and the Ashina, as an animistic tribe, believe that humans had three souls, one in the head, one in the heart and one in the stomach. It was a common shamanic belief that blood is also a vessel for these human souls to connect to each other, to travel both inside and out of the body and to be carried as an essence to other places. Blood therefore is seen as highly sacred and a powerful vessel of the soul and spirit essence and something not to be feared, but revered.

The Ashina clan have passed down stories of the time when humankind first became self-aware and learned that they had souls. The clan believed that their ancestors were the first humans to ask the question: why am I here? And in asking that one question, they separated themselves from nature as unique and although separate from the animals around them, they still formed part of their spirit essence. They were the original humans who first became self-aware. Humans appear to be the only living beings on Earth to possess this faculty, since animals do not ask themselves the fundamental questions that define self-awareness such as what the meaning of life is – and so remain indifferent to the question of their 'being'. This is one of the reasons why the Ashina Clan believed they were the children of the Grey She-Wolf, as some consider that the wolf displays behaviour that indicates it is the only non-human animal to have such 'self-awareness' in the same way as humans. It is widely believed that wolves howl to the night sky as a form of social bonding and as a warning to rivals to keep out of their territory. However, it is also said the howl of the wolf is not just for any survival or evolutionary purpose, but is more of an existential expression of sadness, yearning and puzzlement at being alive.

The prehistoric shamanic peoples of Lake Baikal observed a cosmic system that comprised three worlds: the sky world, the middle world and the Underworld. The middle world is the realm where the Underworld and sky world meet and for human spirits to co-exist in the cycle of their life with animals. The spirits of all herd and plant-eating animals originate in the middle world.

The Underworld is the place where the spirits of the 'animals of blood' originate. These are animals that are carnivorous and have supernal abilities, senses and special powers, such as snakes, cats, bats, corvids and wolves. These animals traverse between the two worlds at will without incarnation and can command and carry other spirits and spirit messages from the world below to the world above.

The sky world is the realm of air, light and storm spirits, rather than animals, and the place of the human afterlife in the stars. From the sky world human souls originate and are brought to and from incarnation by the spirits of birds of prey, such as the eagle and falcon, or by migrating waterfowl such as the swan and goose. Sometimes, however, they can reach the middle world from the lower world through the aid of 'animals of blood' such as the wolf.

The clan story says that a very long time ago, on a night when the heavens stood still on the midsummer solstice, a she-wolf came to the world above from the world below. She had been called by the sound of a distant song. And she had followed the sound from her world deep below. She knew not where she was once she emerged from the cave, but she felt she had travelled here because she wanted to answer the song. The she-wolf gazed upon the sky and saw the heavens full of stars and their bright cold light. She heard the song coming from the stars themselves. A sound only the she-wolf could hear. It was a song that spoke to her of a land across the vast dark rift of the cosmos from the place of origins. As she listened, she raised her head and gazed at the starry sky and cried out in sadness and joy to experience such beauty for the first time and yearned to travel back to the place of the origin of all things.

A human man who lived as one of the animals heard her cries. The she-wolf ceased her crying and looked at the man, who had been watching her. She stared into his eyes and the man gazed back into hers and saw within them the shining points of starlight at which she'd just been gazing. As an animal, the man had never looked up at the night sky before. Seeing them for the first time in the eyes of the She-wolf, he beheld the myriad points of light within the depthless black void of nothing. In that moment the man understood that he had come from there and that he had this starlight inside him, without which he would also be nothing.

The she-wolf told the man her name, 'Aa Shee Na', which meant 'the first of below'. Ashina told him that the light inside him was called the 'sul' and would bestow upon him great powers to travel through the cosmos himself, where great secrets and unfathomable knowledge awaited him. She instructed him to hold onto her tail, which he did. Then she climbed up into the night sky, eventually to travel along the Milky Way back to the place of the source.

From their eventual union the Ashina Clan was created.

This story illustrates how the she-wolf's gifts to humans were knowledge of their soul and self-awareness of their own Being and the question of the meaning of life.

Another legend tells of a young boy who survived a battle in which all of his people were killed. He had been hidden in a marsh for safety but had been injured. Lying helpless, he was discovered by a she-wolf, who took him to her lair and nursed him back to health. Here she raised him alongside her own cubs. Later the boy and the wolf became lovers. Forced to escape her enemies, the she-wolf and her family fled across the sea to a range of mountains, and here she gave birth to ten male children, who were half wolf, half human. In this way, she initiated the Ashina Clan, having granted her children the ability to shape-shift between wolf and human forms. One of Ashina's sons was named Asena, and he eventually took on the role of clan leader. His people became very powerful and ruled the lands around them. To this day, some shamans of Siberia are said to be able to take on the form of a wolf. (Incidentally, the great Mongol leader Genghis Khan claimed direct descent from the Ashina wolf clan. Popular legend asserts that, following his death, the Great Khan's remains were interred within a sacred place called Shaman's Cave, located on Olkhon Island in Lake Baikal).

Ashina is the mother of the shamanic people of Siberia, who first domesticated the wolf. Not simply because she symbolically gave birth to them but because she awakened the awareness that they possessed immortal souls as their connection with creation. This understanding of their soul was how she bestowed them with their great shamanic powers. Powers that resulted from learning to harness their spirit force to commune with and command the forces of earth and sky. Symbolically, Ashina is the mother of consciousness itself, everyone's human soul.

There are different kinds of shamanism in Siberia – among them what are known as white, black and yellow. The white and black are part of the original prehistoric shamanic system, whereas the yellow annexes rituals and practices of the much later Buddhism, which was first introduced during the 13th-14th centuries. Animistic shamans do not adhere to dualistic moralities such as good and evil in their symbolism of black or white, and light and dark. The black and white therefore, while referring to 'terrifying' and 'benevolent' respectively, don't indicate the character of the shamans who espouse these practices, but the nature of the spirits over whom they have command. Some spirits are considered very dangerous indeed and only the most powerful shamans can control them.

You may approach Ashina in order to find and face your true self – the ancestral self, passed down through your genes, which connects you with the first humans who became self-aware. Ashina can be seen as the mother of the human soul.

Meeting Ashina

Deborah Cartwright

Begin the pathworking by entering the Garden of Gateways. To meet with Ashina, you will go into the northern part of the garden. (This is not part of shamanic tradition of Siberia, nor that Ashina is seen as a goddess of the north, but simply to include her and your meeting with her in the most appropriate area of the Garden.)

Follow the path to the north of the garden. It is nighttime, and you walk through a dense pine forest. You can glimpse the sky between the towering trees and can see it is spangled with stars. The landscape of the garden feels wilder than it has on previous visits – older – and as if it is part of a much more rugged and prehistoric landscape.

Eventually, you emerge from the tree-line and find yourself at the foot of a mountain. You can see a rough track leading upwards and begin to climb it. Now the sky blazes with stars above you and you can see the Milky Way clearly. Within it is the Dark Rift, the starry road back to the source of all creation. When you look up you can also see the full red moon of a lunar eclipse. It begins to pulse and look like a beating, bloodied heart. After what seems like a lifetime of walking, you come upon a stone cliff face with a cave entrance in it. The entrance is quite round, almost a circle. Outside the entrance is a tall pile of blue-grey stones in a tubular conical shape. This is an Oobo, or spirit house for the spirit that is the guardian of this entrance to the Underworld. Upon the stones are dark stains of a substance you instinctively know to be blood. You now ask permission of the spirit inside the Oobo to pass and enter into this sacred place. (If you wish, you may visualise giving a symbolic offering of blood to the guardian spirit.)

As you enter the cave, you walk down a curving narrow tunnel, and here you have to bend down a little, in order not to hit your head on the ceiling. There are many other passageways leading off, and you know instinctively which to follow. You can hear faintly the sound of running water. At first, the tunnels are lit by a strange greenish light but as you progress into the mountain, the light becomes dimmer, until you are feeling your way along in almost total darkness.

Then the tunnel opens out into a vast cavern that resembles a natural cathedral, where lies a dark, still lake that fills almost all the cavern. The immense chamber around you is like the hollow interior of a volcano. Looking up, you see it is open to the sky though a hole in the cave ceiling, and the light of the stars and the moon blazes down, illuminating the scene with a spectral glow. You're aware this is an ancient and sacred place.

The lake is of primordial waters, where the spirits of all things of ancient times were born. Aware of this mythical history, you stand facing the primal waters. The lake is still but shining luminously in the silvery blue radiance from the moon. In its centre is a rocky island and here you see that a huge silver she-wolf with a blue-black mane is sitting. It is Ashina. Even from this distance you can perceive that her eyes are the brightest blue; they shine brilliantly. You're aware that the she-wolf contains within herself all the spirits that are waiting to rise up to the middle world.

Ashina compels you to look into the still surface of the lake and scry to see the ghosts of her people, the memories of the rites her female shamans performed many millennia ago. A time when the world was new, and humans had just separated themselves from the animals. You see a circle of women kneeling upon the floor of the cavern. They are dressed in wolf skins and birds' wings, and their bodies are covered in a deep-red ochre paint. They surround the form of another woman who lies stretched out on the cave floor. This woman does not have any pigment on her skin and hair like the others do. Because of this, she is paler and easier to see in the dim moonlight. She appears to be asleep, or in some sort of trance. Her eyes are not closed but have rolled back into her head. You see that the shamans around her are covering her in an unguent, which is an oily paste. The air becomes fragrant with its scent. You feel a distinct urge to draw near and be part of the circle, but instead you must simply observe from a time far in the future of when this event took place.

You realise you are witnessing a sacred rite for women, and that it is going to involve a birth. Yet none of the women are pregnant. The women chant guttural incantations, which rise in pitch. You lose awareness of how long you have been there, how much time has passed, but you are able to hear strange cries and sounds that resound up and around the chamber and from deep underneath the ground. The voices flow past you in fragile echoes and whispers, as if they are being carried by the sound of the rushing underground water.

Suddenly the women stop the incantations and one of them leans over the prone woman. With a small black stone tool, swiftly and neatly she cuts into the woman's inner arms in a straight vertical line from wrist to elbow. In an instant, the other women swiftly bend down and begin to drink the blood that is flowing freely from her opened veins.

You do not feel shocked or horrified by this act but understand that it is a natural part of the rite to birth a new spirit from the world below to the world above. The woman lying in trance is doing something great for the tribe: she is going to be reborn as a different spirit, an ancient one. Something powerful, something needed by her people, which will help guide them in their migration to new lands. The blood-drinking women are draining her life-force to bring her to a near-death state, from which she can be reborn as another spirit. The blood carrying this life force is sacred and must be shared; it cannot be wasted. It cannot be poured into – or drunk from – a vessel or bowl either. It cannot be allowed to see any air, so that the woman's three souls leave her body and enter straight into the protection of the other women around her. Watching this, you begin to taste the metallic tang of blood in your own mouth, as if you were part of this archaic rite.

You can feel the life-force ebbing away from the woman now and can see the soul energies inside her as three balls of light within her body: one in her head and two spiralling around and up and down the central pillar of her spine. The lights seem to grow dimmer until one of the twin spiralling lights extinguishes. At that moment, the women lift her body and place it into the water. You think she must be dead and has been a sacrifice, but then the shamans utter further incantations: 'Shun Mani Tu Tan Ka' – *we call to the spirit of the wolf, up from the world below to the world above.*

The shamans then pull the woman out of the water and lay her on the cave floor once more. She is no longer bleeding, and her skin has turned a shade of blue, which shines with a mineral-like reflection. She breathes heavily, then kneels upright within the circle. Slowly, she raises her head and releases a long and eerie sound, like the whining yawn of a large dog that is almost howling. You can see that she also has clear and bright blue eyes with a black ring around the iris. They are not her eyes anymore, but the eyes of the she-wolf that has come from the world below.

The spirit summoned into the body of this shaman has lived ten thousand lives in the middle world before. It has experienced the self-realisation of death in the Underworld and the sky-world many times and remembers what it found there. It has always been a wolf; it was the only spirit who had ever lived in all three worlds.

Your inner sight is now drawn up from the scrying surface of the lake, across the waters back to Ashina on the island. The she-wolf is powerful but benign. You look into her eyes, and at first all you can see is the reflection of stars within them. Take a moment to feel the presences of the different spirits Ashina carries within her, which are awaiting birth in the upper world – spirits of plants, animals, fish and birds. Commune with them.

Now, the image in Ashina's eyes changes. You see a face looking back at you and realise it is you who is reflected in those shining blue eyes. In a flash, you become aware you're standing once more upon the shore of the lake, quite some distance from the island. When you glance around, you see that the lake has also become like a mirror – but black as obsidian, a vast scrying glass within which you have gazed already and witnessed her clan performing their rites. And now you are reflected there also.

Gaze at your own reflection. Face what you see and go with the first image that comes to you. Don't try and force this process, or attempt to invent an image, or warp what you see to show what you *want* to look like rather than what you are. Let the experience flow.

Speak to Ashina and ask her to tell you the secrets of your true self. Perhaps these are things you have shied away from or fear to face. Now, confront all these things, knowing that facing and being aware of them diminishes any negative power they have over you.

Ashina now tells you to walk across the water to her. You must have courage to do this, because you've no idea whether the water will support you or whether you'll sink and drown, or else fall into an endless void. But Ashina encourages you without words. You must take a leap of faith and overcome the fear of ending, the fear of pain and the fear of death. This is not easy, but the courage exists within you, as does the belief the Earth Water can be your path.

Taking a step onto the black surface is like stepping into your shadow self. Below your feet are many images of your life and experiences that show you truths you might have hidden or denied. Voices clamour around you, but you are undeterred. You carry on walking and the water is like a path of cold glass.

Eventually, you reach the island and here you commune with Ashina for some minutes. She shows you your innermost self, aspects from which you've been displaced and have been searching for. Aspects that are ancient and come from the time before when the human soul was not disconnected from the animal world and from nature. Within you, and now within your reach, is the meaning you couldn't find. You become aware of who and what you really are, the purpose in your life and why you exist.

Then Ashina tells you to hold onto her tail, because she will take you to the stars with her, to the sky world where the spirits of your kind originated. You do as she instructs, and Ashina launches herself upwards, bounding along an invisible path, up and up towards the stars. You hold on to her tail tightly, flying behind her. Ashina takes you to the Wolf's Road, the Dark Rift of the Milky Way, and here you experience the sky world in your own way. You have passed from the world below to the world above. You walk the starry road to the place of life and death. Take some time to see what comes to you as you travel this road.

When you are ready to conclude the pathworking, Ashina takes you back to the middle world of Earth, to an island in the centre of a sacred lake. As you say your goodbyes to Ashina the mother wolf, you realise that you have witnessed the archaic magical secrets of the powerful spirit shamans of early civilisation. A culture that will be remembered as the Gods. For you are just a human, who has traversed to the world below and the world above and will remember what they found there.

Return to the garden by visualising the central tree clearly. This is your beacon and your guide. Be aware that a part of yourself remained there while you were travelling. It was and is your anchor. Return to that part of yourself simply by thinking this. You then find yourself standing beneath the tree, feeling calm and refreshed. Return to normal consciousness and open your eyes.

Dark Mothers

Adapted from a vintage illustration

The Fearsome Dame

To most people, the word mother conjures feelings of safety, nurturing and protection – of love. But for the less fortunate, mothers are not perfect loving beings – they might neglect their offspring, or cause physical pain, or inflict emotional cruelty.

In pagan belief systems, goddesses mirror these aspects of the mother: the nurturer and the monster. Some female spirits or goddesses might even have been termed Mother simply in the hope of appeasing them, averting their displeasure. Mother is used as a term of respect and subservience, like the title Lady, in the same way that the most dangerous and capricious of fairy folk were called in some traditions 'The Good People'.

But perhaps some entities that first appear to be monsters are rather more than that. They personify the indifferent implacability of Nature – the mother of all, yet far from sentimental or affectionate. Her lessons can be harsh, but even so she maintains the role of protectress, of enabling the continuation of life.

A recurring motif in such goddesses is that they have two forms – a beautiful young woman and a hideous crone. She is likely to show you her beautiful side if you please her. When she's angry, she's terrible to behold. This again mirrors Nature – the violence of storms followed by the inexpressible loveliness of a fair summer's day. The dark mother will aid you, but only if she finds you worthy.

Berchta as the Snow Maiden by Danielle Lainton

Berchta
The White Wife

> *'In the sheltered heart of the clumps*
> *last year's foliage still clings to the lower branches,*
> *tatters of orange that mutter with the passage of the wind,*
> *the talk of old women warning the green generation*
> *of what they, too, must come to when the sap runs back.'*
>
> *- Jacquetta Hawkes*

Originally, Berchta, (also known as Perchta and Berchte), was a Teutonic earth goddess, who over the years acquired different forms and interpretations. She became especially associated with winter and its festival period. While essentially benign, she could be capricious and vengeful if people disregarded her preferences and customs. Berchta has the flavour of an old fairy-tale creature, appearing in different forms, sometimes granting boons, other times bringing injury or death. She is the spirit of winter, the *'weisse frau'* or 'white wife'. She has similarities to other goddesses associated with winter, such as Holda and Mother Holle. At the time of year when she roamed the forests and fields, people would leave out offerings of food and drink for her. One of her epithets was 'guardian of the beasts'.

The meaning of her name is not known for certain; it could mean 'brightness' or 'hidden/covered'. She has two distinct forms. In one, she is a beautiful pale maiden, bright as snow, her long flaxen hair worn in a plait that hangs down her back. She is clothed in white robes, with her snow-pale face partially concealed by a veil that extends down to her gown. In complete contrast, her other form is that of a hag, who has very bright eyes but an ancient wrinkled face. Her long grey hair is straggly and her nose large and hooked. She carries a staff and her garments are shabby and ragged.

In both aspects, Berchta is said to have one deformed foot. This, in some legends, is described as disproportionately long and flat, perhaps fashioned that way by the treadle of her incessant spinning – since she has strong associations with that occupation. In other accounts, she is known as having a swan's or goose's foot. This suggests she was a shapeshifter, a swan or goose maiden, whose human body still retained a part of her animal form. There are several old fairy stories, from different European countries, which feature a character with a deformed foot, whose name derives from regional renditions of Bertha (a form of Berchta). And, traditionally, one of the ways a fairy woman could be identified was through having bird's feet – a fact she would go to pains to conceal.

Although undoubtedly of earlier origins than Christianity, Berchta remained as a supernatural or fairy creature in common folklore into the Christian era. She was said to walk the land between Christmas and Epiphany, and on Twelfth Night would direct her attention to children, and the younger servants of a household. Nothing could be hidden from Berchta, and she would know who had been good over the past year, and who had been bad or had shirked their duties. If their behaviour came up to her standards, Berchta would reward them with a silver coin, which they'd discover in a shoe or a pail the next day, but if she perceived bad or lazy behaviour, she would slit open their stomachs and gut them, replacing their entrails with pebbles and straw. In this way, she was a bringer of death.

As she was particularly connected with spinning, she was said to be concerned about whether young girls had spun enough wool or flax over the year. If they didn't come up to scratch, the penalty, as we've learned, was severe.

Berchta was used as a kind of 'bogey woman' to frighten children – and perhaps gullible young servants – into good behaviour. And it was clearly the parents and householders who slipped silver coins into the shoes and pails of those who'd been judged well, although not going so far as to cut open miscreants and stuff them with straw!

Berchta had an entourage of winter spirits known as the *Perchten*, which is the plural form of Perchta, one of the variations of her name. *Perchten* also applies to the strange animal masks that even to this day are worn at seasonal festivals and parades among the Austrian Alps. Similar to how Berchta had two forms, there were two kinds of follower (or mask), as well. Like their mistress, they would reward the good and punish the bad. The 'beautiful *Perchten*' or '*Schönperchten*' in the local language, brought luck and wealth to all. But the 'ugly *Perchten*' or '*Schiachperchten*' had hideous faces with huge tusks and fangs. They were rough and hairy and had horses' tails. They lacked ears so they couldn't hear the screams of those they tormented. They were so frightening, even ghosts and demons would flee from them in terror. It was a custom for men to dress up as these ugly *Perchten*, wearing wooden painted masks, and go around the local community, from house to house, to drive out evil spirits.

In Austria, the customs and rites of Berchta continue to survive, and have been absorbed into the tourist industry in ski resorts and other towns, where colourful *Perchten* ceremonies and costumes have become popular winter attractions.

Meeting Berchta

Begin the pathworking by entering the Garden of Gateways. To meet with Berchta, you will go into the northern part of the garden.

Take the appropriate exit from the centre of the garden and follow the path to the cave in the north. As soon as you cross the threshold of the first chamber, the air grows cold and your breath steams before you. You pass quickly through the cave and along a straight passageway, to emerge into a new landscape.

You find yourself standing on a narrow track in the centre of an immense forest in winter time. The trees around you are both evergreen and deciduous, their branches weighed down with heavy snow. The scene around you is completely still and silent, somewhat unnerving.

You begin to walk along the path, heading in a northerly direction. Gradually, you become aware of creatures rustling and skittering in the undergrowth around you, not quite seen, but heard. They don't draw close to you, but you're aware of their presence. You realise these are the *Perchten*, Berchta's magical attendants.

Suddenly, a large, black goat appears on the path in front of you. He has six horns: four jutting upwards and two more curling around his head. He has a long red tongue, which lolls from his mouth, and you feel somewhat wary of him. He simply stands upon the path and stares at you from yellow eyes. You're not sure what to do or how to take this presence. Eventually, you move towards him. At this point, the goat turns round and darts away along the path. You see him pause further up the track, turning to look at you again. You realise he's leading you and you follow. The goat pauses three times to allow you to catch up, then you emerge into a clearing among the trees. The goat disappears into the forest once more.

You see a female form standing in front of you – Berchta, in her aspect of the hag, carrying a gnarled wooden staff. She's frightful to behold, having a twisted face with a huge nose. She has six horns, like the goat, and is dressed in black rags. This is the aspect of Berchta who judges our actions throughout the year. If you seek advancement in life, have you done all that you could to help achieve that? Or have you expected others to carry you, or waited for fortune to stumble upon you by accident? Berchta's message is that we need to have fertile ground in which to plant the seeds of future success. We should care for the tender green shoots and help them grow. If neglected, they will wither away. Once you nurture your own growth, Berchta will help you and bring fortune to you.

Spend some moments thinking about changes you could make to your life or your attitude that will assist such growth.

Once you have mulled over your situation in this way, with total honesty, Berchta transforms before your eyes into a beautiful young woman, her maiden aspect. You can't help but feel relief at this, because it's easier to connect with the fearsome Berchta when she takes this form. She's like a snow maiden, fashioned of snow rather than flesh and blood. As you gaze upon her, snow begins to fall around and upon you. The soft flakes feel like caresses against your skin. You gaze upon Berchta and realise the snow is somehow coming from her, as well as the cold air that is growing gradually chillier. You know you won't be able to stay here long, but you sense it's important to connect with Berchta for a while.

Her strange ice-blue gaze compels you to stare into her eyes. As you do so, you feel as if your body is turning to solid ice. But you realise this is a good thing, because this process will capture and freeze any negativity that might have become attached to you over the years. It will purge you of negative energies or parasites, of which you might not even have been aware.

This negativity is like a gang of bad spirits, sniggering and skittering around you. They want to avoid capture, so they may continue to plague you. But now Berchta's *Schiachperchten* appear, the ugly spirits. They're so frightening, the parasites are frozen in terror, and quickly become trapped within the ice. Soon, their chittering is stopped for good.

After a minute or so, you look away from Berchta, which breaks the spell. At once, the ice within and upon you begins to crack and melt, until it falls from your body. Any negativity that's held you back, or has leeched your energy, is also falling from you. You experience a profound sense of relief and unburdening.

When you look at the goddess once more, she's resumed her hag form, but she smiles benevolently at you. Her eyes are very bright and filled with humour. She strikes the ground with her staff and the *Schönperchten*, the beautiful spirits, appear. They fly around you, showering you with white sparks, like snowflakes, which you know bring good fortune. The goddess has smiled upon you and you realise that the concepts of beautiful and ugly are only skin deep. The time has come for you to leave.

Return to the garden by visualising the central tree clearly. This is your beacon and your guide. Be aware that a part of yourself remained there while you were travelling. It was and is your anchor. Return to that part of yourself simply by thinking this. You find yourself standing beneath the tree, feeling calm and refreshed. Return to normal consciousness and open your eyes.

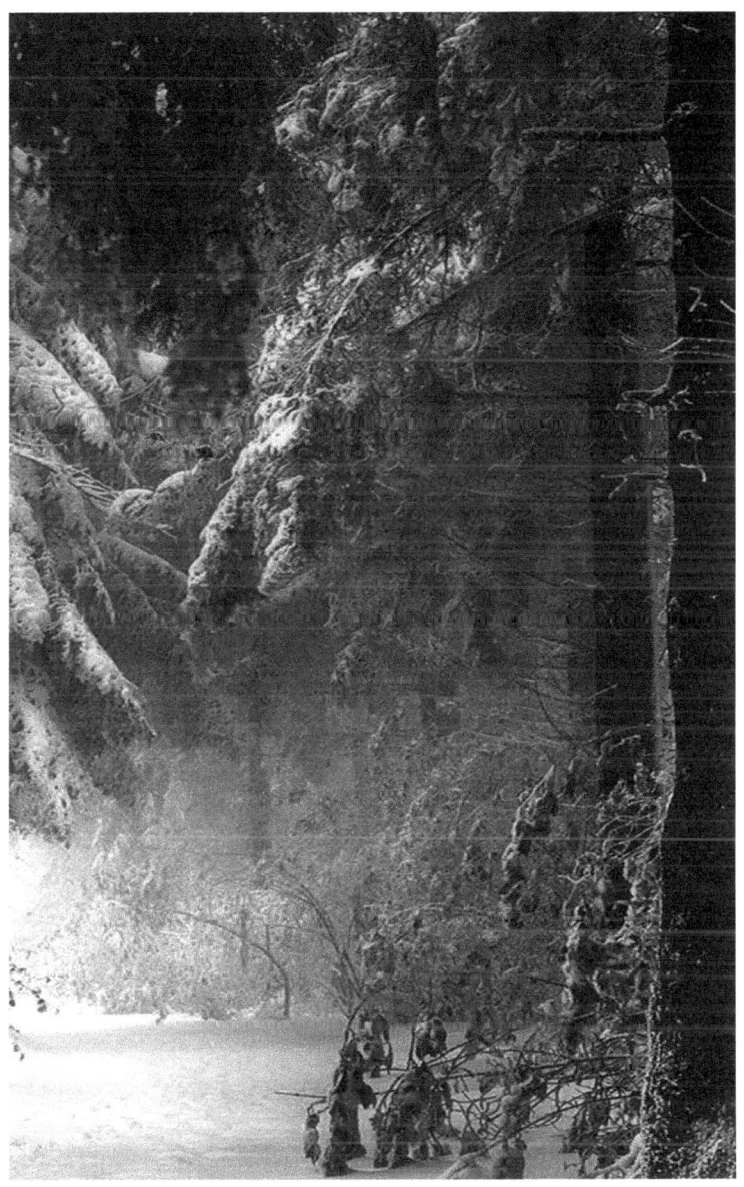

Berchta's Realm by Storm Constantine

Traditional illustration of Smashana Kali in the Cremation Grounds, standing upon Shiva, surrounded by vicious female spirits

Kali
The Beautiful Black Devourer

She is all beauty –
This woman nude and terrible and black,
Who tells the name of God on the skulls of the dead,
Who creates the bloodshed on which demons fatten,
Who slays rejoicing and repents not,
And blesses him only that lies crushed beneath Her feet.
Her mass of black hair flows behind Her like the wind,
Or like time 'the drift and passage of all things'.
She is blue almost to blackness, like a mighty shadow,
And bare like the dread realities of life and death.

From *Kali the Mother*, Sister Nivedita,
(Advaits Ashrama, 1986)

Even if people are unaware of the deities of the Hindu belief system, they've often heard of the dark mother Kali – or Kali Ma – and are familiar with her image: naked or semi-naked, with multiple arms wielding weapons, and wearing a necklace of severed heads. Her name derives from a word meaning 'black' or 'dark-coloured', and she is generally depicted with night-black or midnight-blue skin and extremely long, wild black hair. Her name is also associated with a word that means time, or 'the fulness (or force) of time', and this has been said to mean she represents the cycle of time itself, the processes in nature from birth to death and decay, and presumably to rebirth.

Kali has appeared in movies and fiction many times and in many guises, as have the secret societies formed in her name. There are few people who don't know the term 'thug', or what it means – generally a violent, ignorant person – but it's doubtful many are aware that this word derives from a secret cult of Kali devotees – the thugees. She has a reputation of being blood-thirsty and merciless. And yet still she is the Great Mother, and supposedly a creature of beguiling beauty – a fascinating goddess of contradictions.

Kali is one of the consorts of the beautiful god, Shiva, and is often shown in artistic representations trampling upon his prone body. Shiva appears to accept this position calmly, almost as if he's swooning in pleasure – the image doesn't convey violence, even if it does suggest great power. One myth tells us that Shiva deliberately put himself beneath Kali's feet in order to calm her, when she'd been overcome by bloodlust during a slaughter of demons. In other representations, Kali is depicted dancing with Shiva, or joined in sexual union with him. These deities are intricately connected. Shiva cannot manifest without Kali, and she cannot exist without him. She's said to be a manifestation of Shiva's power. She is the destroyer, the mistress of dissolution, yet also a mother goddess, albeit a fearsome one. She maintains the order of the universe, and in her role of destroyer purges ignorance.

The goddess's appearance in most depictions are horrifying. She's always shown with multiple arms; usually four or ten. Each hand holds something of spiritual or magical significance, or else makes a meaningful gesture. She might wield a combination of a sword, a sickle-shaped blade, a bow and arrow, a small axe, a spear or a trident, or all of them. She is generally represented as gripping in one hand the severed head of a demon by the hair, with another hand holding a bowl beneath it to catch the blood. She may carry a basin of fire or a lotus, or other items of religious significance. Or she might simply hold one or more hands in a *mudra*, a symbolic position of the hand and fingers. Her bright red tongue is usually shown lolling from her mouth and is abnormally long. Sometimes, her wide mouth bristles with small tusks or fangs. In many representations, she wears a necklace of skulls or severed heads, and a girdle of similar grisly trophies, or else severed arms. Her wild eyes stare balefully, often red with rage. Gazing upon an image of her, you know in your bones she is not a goddess to be trifled with or crossed. And yet this terrible Kali does have a benign aspect as a protector. Her aggression isn't mindless or random; she punishes evil.

Kali is less ferocious in her form of Kali Ma – the creator, the mother, who is a nature goddess. This is probably her most popular aspect within common Hinduism. In this calmer manifestation, she is depicted as standing serenely upon Shiva – rather than what looks like trampling him – and symbolises the preservation of the natural world. Her rippling black hair that flows so abundantly represents nature free from human civilisation. In this form too, her blackness represents the eternal night before creation; everything was born from this darkness. If she is shown with blue skin, this can be seen as representing the blue of the sea and the sky.

Nature is impartial, sometimes dangerous, sometimes benign. Kali encapsulates this idea. She encompasses within her being the creator, the nurturer, the devourer and the preserver. There are many interpretations and stories associated with Kali in the Hindu tradition – far too many to list here. It's almost disorientating to think that the huge rituals, or *pujas*, performed to Kali in India today, attended by thousands and thousands of people, are essentially the same as they were when the pharaohs ruled in Egypt, and goddesses such as Isis and Sekhmet were worshipped. Their time passed beneath the sands, revived only by modern practitioners drawn to these neglected goddesses. But Kali is eternal, unchanged, still surrounded by adoring followers as she was thousands of years ago. She's complex and ancient, and has many different forms and epithets, but always she is – at her core – the Black One, the Dark Mother.

According to various scholars who have studied this powerful goddess, Kali has at least thirty different forms, some of them quite specialised, such as Dakait Kali, the goddess of thieves. Shyama Kali is a domestic goddess, who is kind, grants favours and dispels fear. Rakha Kali is a protectress, who is called upon in times of catastrophe, such as during floods, famines, natural disasters and epidemics. Nitya Kali banishes disease and suffering, while Phalaharini Kali has the power to change the consequences of a person's actions – in this sense, to rectify mistakes. To the Tantrics, Siddha Kali was the aspect to turn to when seeking perfection, to become perfect.

In this book, the pathworking leads to Kali's most ferocious form, Smashana Kali, the embodiment of the power of destruction. The reason for this concerns the beliefs of the Tantrics, specifically that shying away from the unpleasant or frightening aspects of life restricts one's spiritual progress, for to imagine the goddess simply as a benign mother is to deny her complex nature, her many forms. The cremation grounds (known as *ghats*) illustrate harsh realities and the transience of life; if a person fears these things, they should face them. Yet against this charnel scene, Smashana Kali stands fearless and triumphant, ready to smite ignorance and evil. She's surrounded by corpses, symbols of death, and by jackals who eat the dead, and terrifying female spirits. The goal is to see past these symbols to the raw beauty of the goddess. Respect her, brave what she reveals, and she will set you upon a stronger path in life.

Meeting Kali

Begin the pathworking by entering the Garden of Gateways. To meet with Kali, you will go into the southern part of the garden, to seek its aspect of fire and heat.

Take the appropriate exit from the centre of the garden and follow the path to the southern gateway.

You find yourself in the land of India, as the sun begins to set. You're following a road towards the sunset, with forest to either side. The air is still very hot. As you walk, you notice shrines to Kali beside the path. These are dedicated to the goddess in her benign and tender aspects. Offerings of flowers, fruit and incense have been left for her, and the cult images in the shrines depict a beautiful, blue-skinned woman with flowing black hair. Although her tongue might poke from her mouth, and she's adorned with the skulls and severed limbs of her fiercer aspects, she smiles benignly, and has the appearance almost of a young, innocent girl dressing up in costume.

You are not here to seek this aspect of Kali. You have put away earthly desires and concerns and have the courage to face the goddess in her most severe aspect: Kali Smashana, goddess of the cremation grounds.

The sky ahead of you has become a deep, burning red, and the sun an immense ruby globe, shimmering as it sinks into the horizon. You see ahead of you the gateway to a vast cremation ground or *ghat*, where the dead are burned. The gates are enormous and elaborate, fashioned of stone and covered in intricate carvings. The stone was clearly once white but has become blackened over the years by the soot from burning corpses. Walls lead away from north and south into the distance. Already, even before you enter the grounds, the air is full of floating motes of ash and smoke. You pass beneath the gate and gaze upon the spreading burning grounds ahead of you. There are many buildings, in the same elaborate architectural style as the gates, but these structures are scattered widely. Despite their grandeur they seem dwarfed by their setting. Between the buildings, there is a host of pyres where bodies burn, but mainly there is open ground, which beneath your feet is littered with gnawed bones and grey-black, greasy ash.

Buildings Within Vyas Chatri, an Old Indian Cremation Ground

Wild dogs are running about investigating the charred ground, seeking bones to gnaw upon, while vultures and crows pick at any flesh they find. The air is sweet yet foul with the smell of burned meat and blood. You have to tie a scarf over the lower half of your face to aid your breathing as you proceed. Now, you become aware of a strange keening sound and are drawn towards it.

A bright, fiery glow can be glimpsed between the buildings ahead. You go towards this and emerge into a kind of arena or shallow pit. In the centre of this area, a fire roars high, filling the air with sparks and smoke. The ground itself here is burning, but you can walk through the flames without them harming you. Before the central fire stands Kali, an immense, overpowering presence. She is surrounded by a chanting crowd of terrifying female spirits, who have wild hair and eyes and wield swords and daggers. They dance around the goddess, uttering their chaotic song to her. They pay no attention to you.

You come to stand in front of Kali and unwind the scarf from your face as a gesture of respect to her, an acknowledgement of her meaning and that you are not afraid of it. No matter how the air might sting you with its heat and sparks, or fill your nose with the stench of death, you are prepared to face it. Kali is terrible but wonderful, her tongue lolling out, her hands brandishing weapons, as well as her symbolic artefacts. Beneath her feet, Shiva, more beautiful than can be imagined, swoons upon the ground, his hair spreading over it.

As you gaze upon the goddess, you are aware that she represents the unifying power of creation, beyond dualities. In her, all opposites exist and yet do not exist at all. She is like fire, which can warm the home and cook our food, but can also rage across a country destroying everything in its path. The fire is neither good nor evil: it simply is, its raw, pure self. As is Kali. She is the Kind Mother and the Terrifying Mother. She has the ability to create and nurture, but also to kill and ruin. She is Nature itself.

Gaze into Kali's eyes and she will purge you of ignorance. This will clear the path towards your future progress: spiritually, mentally and physically. Imagine that the fire of the cremation grounds rises all around you, but does not burn your flesh. All it burns is those aspects of yourself you wish to shed. You want to know your raw, true self, beyond artifice or self-delusion.

Experience this as fully as you can imagine it.

After you have experienced this cleansing, tell Kali that you also seek insight and knowledge of her deeper mysteries. You ask her if there's anything you need to know, either about your own life or about the inner mysteries of her tradition, and about the world from which they came. When you are ready to depart, bow to Kali and bid her farewell.

Return to the garden by visualising the central tree clearly. This is your beacon and your guide. Be aware that a part of yourself remained there while you were travelling. It was and is your anchor. Return to that part of yourself simply by thinking this. You find yourself standing beneath the tree, feeling calm and refreshed. Return to normal consciousness and open your eyes.

Based upon an old woodcut of Calcutta

Sedna by Danielle Lainton

Sedna
Vengeful Mother of the Sea

> *The fishermen know that the sea is dangerous*
> *and the storm terrible,*
> *but they have never found these dangers*
> *sufficient reason for remaining ashore.*
>
> Vincent Van Gogh

Sedna is a goddess of the Inuit people, who live in the extreme northern areas of the world, such as Arctic Canada, Greenland and Siberia. The Inuit rely upon the sea for its bounty, especially its animals, and in the old legends Sedna was Mother of the Sea. There are many different versions of a myth that feature Sedna. These stories share a recurrent theme: Sedna loses her fingers, which fall into the sea and turn into the marine creatures prized and hunted by the Inuit – seals, whales, walruses and other creatures of the deep.

In one story, Sedna is the daughter of the creator-god Anguta. She is a giant, and tortured continually by raging, insatiable hunger, so much so she even attacks her own parents. Furious, Anguta drags her to his kayak and takes her out to sea, where he throws her overboard, intent on ridding his family of her. Sedna clings to the side of the boat by her fingers, but despite her pleas for mercy, Anguta chops off her fingers so she can't hang on. She sinks into the ocean, but instead of drowning transforms into a mighty sea goddess.

In a slightly different version of this story, Sedna rejects all the suitors her parents find for her and, to their disgust (and most likely in indignant protest), elects instead to marry a dog. As in the previous tale, her angry father throws her into the sea, and her attempts to cling to his boat are thwarted by him cutting off her fingers.

Yet another version of this story paints Sedna as an orphan who is mistreated by her community. So strong is their desire to be rid of her that they too carry her out to sea, only to cut off her fingers as she tries to save herself by clinging to the boat that carried her.

There are many alternative tellings of this legend across Inuit communities, and several of them involve birds. In some of these, Sedna isn't the daughter of a god, but simply a beautiful human maiden. In one example, similar to one of the myths mentioned above, Sedna isn't satisfied by any of the men who seek her hand in marriage – who are hunters from the village. Her parents feel it's time she was married but she rejects everyone. One day, a hunter arrives who is a stranger. Sedna's father, perhaps sick of her contrary ways, offers to give his daughter to the stranger in exchange for fish. To make sure Sedna doesn't cause any trouble, he sedates her before handing her over to the hunter. Sedna is carried by her new spouse to a nest on a cliff-face and here she awakes, finding herself surrounded by birds. Her new husband reveals to her his true form; he is a bird-spirit. Different variations of the story claim he is a raven, a petrel or a fulmar spirit. Meanwhile, perhaps feeling guilty for what he's done, Sedna's father sets out in his kayak to rescue his daughter. He succeeds in getting her into his boat, but then the bird-spirit realises what has happened. Furious, he conjures a terrible storm. The kayak must surely sink, and in terror Sedna's father throws her overboard, selfishly hoping this will placate the angry bird-spirit and save him from death. Desperately, Sedna clings to the side of the boat, only for her father to chop off her fingers with an axe, before striking her across the head. Senseless, Sedna sinks to the bottom of the sea where her fingers become seals, and she becomes mistress of the ocean's creatures.

All variations of this story end with Sedna's fingers being severed, which become marine creatures. In all of them, Sedna herself sinks to the ocean floor, and transforms into a goddess. Sometimes, she takes on the form of a mermaid by growing a fish's tail.

Sedna is believed to be quite vengeful in nature, perhaps not surprising considering the consistent theme of her myths. Inuit hunters seek always to appease her, so she will not withhold the bounty of the sea, her children. The hunters believe that if they pray to her, she will release her creatures to be hunted.

Should hunting go really badly for a community, the people believe Sedna is angry with them. One way in which this is dealt with is through the help of local shamans. Entering trance, they will, in their visions, transform into a fish and go to visit Sedna at the bottom of the sea. Sedna particularly likes having her hair combed and braided, perhaps because she lacks the fingers to do this herself. The shaman performs this duty to please her, so that in her happier mood she will then send plenty of sea creatures to be hunted.

Meeting Sedna

Begin the pathworking by entering the Garden of Gateways. To meet with Sedna, you will go into the western part of the garden. While Sedna is a northern goddess, in this instance you are focusing upon her association with water.

Take the appropriate exit from the centre and follow the

path to the west. When you reach the semi-circular pool, take the steps that lead down to the right, as you did in your first exploration of the garden. The steps lead you down to the ocean.

When you reach the shore, you find yourself in a cold, northern climate. You are dressed in thick furs, such as an Inuit hunter would wear, with a large hood surrounded by the fur of the arctic fox. There are dark cliffs behind you, hung with icicles. The beach isn't sandy but covered in blue black stones, occasionally draped with sea weed. You notice that nearby is an old black jetty poking out into the turbulent dark waters. A small boat is moored to it.

You approach the boat and climb into it. There is a narrow bench for you to sit on. Of its own accord, the boat begins to push out towards the deep sea, rocking on the choppy waves that heave like immense watery muscles beneath you. It feels as if you're travelling over a living body that is unpredictable and dangerous. Overhead, sea birds swoop across the heavy sky, uttering harsh cries.

After a short while, and once the shore is quite far behind you, the boat comes to a halt. You look over the side and are aware of how deep the waters are beneath you. You stand up in the boat and utter a call, such as the seabirds make. You call in this way to Sedna.

After a few moments, you notice movement within the heaving darkness of the waves and realise that some creature is swimming towards you. As it draws closer, it appears at first to be a mermaid, a woman with a fish's tail, but then when she breaks the surface, you see that it's an Inuit woman. You know that this is Sedna in her human form. Her long, wet black hair hangs over her face, obscuring most of her features. You wonder whether this really is hair because it looks weirdly like seaweed. You can tell that she's staring at you, even though you can't see her eyes. She unnerves you, but you know you must show no fear.

Sedna puts her hands on the side of the boat and you see she has no fingers. She heaves herself upwards and crawls into the boat, with her hair still hanging over her face. Then, she gets to her feet. She wears a garment that moulds to her body. It looks black and slippery like seaweed or wet leather, and is dark in colour, greenish-brown. Sheets of seaweed cling to it.

Sedna pays you no attention, says nothing, but simply goes to the prow of the boat and holds out her arms horizontally. She then bends her elbows, so her forearms point upwards and calls out to the sea. She utters a loud, unearthly call, which resembles the deep, booming call of a whale, blended with the coarse cry of a seabird. The sound makes your skin crawl, for it seems almost as if it doesn't belong in this world.

After a minute or so, Sedna ceases her call and turns to you. She brushes back her wet hair with the heels of her hands. Now you can see her face. She's like a cross between a fish and woman, with round staring eyes. Her mouth is full of long, needle-like teeth, such as fishes that live in the very deepest waters have. Sedna's gaze is challenging, as if she dares you to find her ugly or strange. You do not. In her weird way, she possesses an unearthly beauty and grace.

Now, you're aware of activity in the sea around the boat and realise that sea creatures are approaching from every direction. Sedna leans down and puts her hands in the water, on either side of the boat. The creatures come to her, their dark, supple backs breaking the surface of the water. They swarm around her hands and attach themselves to her with their mouths. Before your eyes, the creatures shrink and change, and become the fingers Sedna lost. In fact, you realise, she never lost them at all. Her fingers are everywhere within the ocean. The creatures that came from them are her children. However, the fingers of her hands now resemble her teeth, long and pointed, the nails like needles. They are webbed, like the fins of a deep-sea fish, who is armed with spines.

Sedna straightens up once more and stares at you. Her eyes are wide and black, and now more than a fish, they resemble the round eyes of a seal. You ask if she will share her mysteries with you. She assents with a nod of her head.

You hold her gaze for as long as possible and through it experience her hidden mysteries, see her realm, the icy land of the northern seas, with its icebergs, seals, polar bears, great auks and other birds and animals that live on the ice and the cliffs. She takes you down beneath the dark waves to her realm below, which she allows you to explore.

Eventually, Sedna releases a piercing, deafening call that summons your spirit back to the boat. She transforms into a raven, which flies off towards land, whose distant cliffs you can just make out through a misty haze. She flies over the top of the cliffs and out of sight.

Return to the garden by visualising the central tree clearly. This is your beacon and your guide. Be aware that a part of yourself remained there while you were travelling. It was and is your anchor. Return to that part of yourself simply by thinking this. You find yourself standing beneath the tree, feeling calm and refreshed. Return to normal consciousness and open your eyes.

Sedna's Sea by Storm Constantine

Babalon by Danielle Lainton

Babalon
Mother of Mystery

*I saw a woman sitting upon a scarlet beast,
having seven heads and ten horns.
And the woman was arrayed in purple and scarlet,
and bedecked with gold and precious stones and pearls,
having a golden cup in her hand full of abominations
and the impurities of her fornication,
And upon her forehead was written a name of mystery,
Mystery, Babylon the Great, Mother of Harlots
and Abominations of the Earth.*

Adapted from the *Book of Revelations, The Bible*

In 1904, infamous British occultist, Aleister Crowley, established the magical system of Thelema. Babalon was a goddess within this system. She was most likely inspired by the description of the Whore of Babylon, in the 'Book of Revelations' of *The Bible*.

The description at the top of this page is very similar to how Crowley describes Babalon. She is depicted as 'Lust' in the major arcana of Crowley's 'Thoth' Tarot deck, riding naked upon the 'Great Beast', her head thrown back in ecstasy. In 'The Book of Thoth' Crowley writes:

'She rides astride the Beast; in her left hand she holds the reins, representing the passion which unites them. In her right, she holds aloft the cup, the Holy Grail aflame with love and death. In this cup are mingled the elements of the sacrament of the Aeon.'

Same being, it would appear, but from a markedly different perspective. Christian writers saw the Whore of

Babylon as a personification of evil and excess, while to Crowley she was one of the great mysteries of life, and integral to the path to enlightenment, in the form of a powerful divine female.

Babalon can be seen as one of the darkest of mother goddesses that humanity have invented, and she has several forms within the Thelemic tradition. She is the Great Mother and also The Gateway to the City of Pyramids. The Great Mother is integral to the Gnostic Mass of the Thelemic system, where she is regarded as the Earth itself, at its most fertile and abundant. Sometimes referred to as the Scarlet Woman, this aspect is Babalon encapsulated in human form, via a priestess, and is distinct from her cosmic abstract self – although most practitioners don't differentiate between them. Babalon is also the 'Mother of Abominations', which is mentioned within a reference to her role as Scarlet Woman:

Let him look upon the cup whose blood is mingled therein, for the wine of the cup is the blood of the saints. Glory unto the Scarlet Woman, Babalon the Mother of Abominations, that rideth upon the Beast, for she hath spilt their blood in every corner of the earth and lo! she hath mingled it in the cup of her whoredom.
  from Crowley's 'The Vision and the Voice' (12th Aethyr):

Crowley was reputed to explore aspects of human nature that were considered very dark, especially in the era in which he lived. This reputation was not wholly justified. In general, Christian Victorian, so-called polite society was riddled with the concepts of shame and sin in respect of sexuality, but Crowley saw nothing wrong with breaking through this hypocrisy. In many ways, he was ahead of his time and was vilified for it.

Goddesses, even within the Neo-Paganism of that time, were mostly either remote, romanticised or unattainable in nature. Babalon, in all her lusty, bloody glory, accessible to all brave enough to seek her favour, showed a side of female divinity that perhaps wasn't widely acknowledged in early modern paganism.

The Scarlet Woman is the 'sacred whore', a representation of female sexuality, free of restraint and full of mysterious power. The term whore is not used as a derogatory term, but because her favours are available, without prejudice or conditions, to anyone. However, there is a high price – life-blood from the magical practitioner who seeks advancement through her. Perhaps even a little of their sanity.

Babalon's role as 'Gateway to the City of the Pyramids' forms part of the lore of Thelema. Simplified, the practitioner's purpose is to work through the system, gaining knowledge and experience as they progress. The penultimate stage of this is attaining 'Knowledge and Conversation with the Holy Guardian Angel'. After this, the adept – as they are known – must undergo a terrifying trial, the final stage to enlightenment.

The City of the Pyramids is the mystical home of those who have completed their spiritual work. To get there, they must cross the Abyss, an arid waste of spiritual dissipation and oblivion. It is a realm of nothingness, devoid of life and energy. In this place dwells Choronzon, a demon who derives originally from the works of the 16th century occultist, Dr. John Dee. Choronzon will attempt to beguile those who enter his realm, so they remain trapped there. And yet, on the other side of the Abyss waits Babalon, beckoning the adept to come to her. She guards the Abyss from the other side yet is also a guide in this instance. When the adept reaches her, they must abandon themselves to her completely – symbolised by an act of spilling their blood into her grail. They become a child within her, to be reborn as a Master of the Temple, who may dwell within the sacred City of the Pyramids as a saint. Blood then is the price the adept must pay Babalon in order to be reborn in a higher state of being.

If we look at what Babalon can symbolise outside of her specific functions within Thelema, she represents the full liberation of femininity and full expression of sexuality. She is therefore a symbol of free will and freedom, an aspect of femininity a woman may experience to release herself from constraint caused by her upbringing and conditioning. It aids a woman to find free expression of her sexuality and empowerment by taking on the role of Babalon. She is the representation of the magnetism and allure that draw people to you. You may draw that energy into your life to feel empowered within your day-to-day world. Babalon is hidden beneath your work clothing, your social dress. She can be turned on within you, as if by a switch, and also turned off in the same way.

    The pathworking to Babalon can be performed at any time of year, but the month of Scorpio is particularly relevant to her and is certainly the time when she should be in your thoughts.

For men, the importance of this pathworking is to recognise the embodiment of the goddess within women. The goddess is the giver of life. Sexuality brings forth life, and it should be celebrated, not hidden away or regarded as shameful. It is beautiful and recognised by the ancients in the cults of goddesses like Ishtar and Venus. One of the forms of Ishtar was Ishara, and she was a scorpion goddess, her animals being the snake and the scorpion, associated with the constellation of Scorpius.

When visiting Babalon you should decide beforehand the character of your visit. Babalon may have different significance for men and women. You can invoke the element of Babalon that feeds the masculine or feminine frequency within the human form and mind. This does not necessarily mean being restricted by one's bodily gender.

Meeting Babalon

Begin the pathworking by entering the Garden of Gateways. To meet with Babalon, you will go into the southern part of the garden, seeking Babalon as a powerful goddess most closely associated with the element of fire.

Take the appropriate exit from the centre of the garden and follow the path to the southern gate. You emerge here, not into a desert or cremation ground, but into a landscape of fields and small clumps of woodland. A wide river runs through it, and you can glimpse the shine of water through the trees, indicating the presence of hidden pools.

As you walk towards the sunset, you see the silhouette of a lone, square tower just beside the road. You're aware that one of the symbols connected with the Whore of Babylon is Babylon itself, and its great Ziggurat, which some believe was the Tower of Babel. This must be the place you have to go to.

By the time you reach the tower, the sun has sunk below the horizon and it's fully dark. There is a wooden door at the base of the tower, carved with strange creatures that seem to be hybrids of many different animals and mythical beings. The door isn't locked and opens silently at your touch.

You enter the tower and see there's a stone spiral stair that leads around the inside to all of its floors. But you're drawn towards a door opposite to you. Again, this opens at your touch.

Beyond the threshold lies a large chamber designed along the lines of an ancient temple, with tall red columns around the walls. The colour scheme is mainly red and white, with some black and hints of green. Oil lamps hang from sconces on the columns, filling the room with a golden glow. Incense burns upon tall braziers and you can discern the scent of roses within it, along with precious resins and other flowers. A dozen or so people sit on cushions on the tiled floor, talking together and drinking. You get the feeling they're waiting for something.

In the centre of the room stands an altar, which bears a bowl of living flame and two golden cups. On the far wall, opposite the entrance to the room, stands a golden throne.

Suddenly, the oil lamps upon the columns grow dim, are almost extinguished. You blink in the unexpected darkness. Then the lamps bloom once more, although not as brightly as before. You can see that the golden throne across the room is now occupied. A woman sits upon it: Babalon, the Great Mother, the Sacred Whore.

She appears as a beautiful, voluptuous woman, who oozes sensuality. She holds a serpent in each hand, which are white with ruby eyes. The serpents seem to dance upon the air, supported by her grasp. Babalon wears a translucent robe of red and white, and you're able to discern the curves of her body through the shimmering fabric. Several veils or scarves are draped over her robe. She wears a golden circlet upon her head, adorned with a crescent moon that hangs over her brow. Her thick red-black hair falls to her breasts.

Everyone in the room has fallen silent and bow their heads to Babalon. Gracefully, she rises slowly from her seat and bends to release the serpents. They form a circle for a moment, and then slither off to the edge of the room and disappear.

You can now hear the music of finger symbols and hand drums. And Babalon begins to dance. She winds like a serpent, her movements the epitome of sensuality and female sexuality. Her perfect feet seem to flicker beneath her robe. She is the essence of beguiling femininity. Her glance is secretive and mysterious. Her hands weave in sacred gestures.

The people in the room now sprawl upon the floor in a circle, providing an arena in which Babalon dances. If you are here to revere Babalon through a masculine aspect, she beckons to you now. She has come to a standstill beside the altar. You go and kneel before her and kiss her feet. You may offer the five-fold kiss of the Wicca belief system, if you so desire. This kiss is to demonstrate your respect for all Babalon symbolises, to revere the principle of creation.

Babalon acknowledges and absorbs your simple but meaningful offering with a gracious yet ecstatic movement of her head. You now lie down before her, your limbs extended.

Babalon begins to dance once more, the movements of her slim feet weaving between your limbs. She removes her veils, one by one, which fall down over you. The seventh veil wafts down to cover your face, so you cannot see. You can feel Babalon's presence very close to you, her energy, her heat, her sexuality. You experience the jolt of a Kundalini-like energy that courses through your body like electricity. You feel aroused. At the same time, you feel a great strength building up within you, which is the essence of the goddess. You realise this embodied power will build your own confidence and strength. You can evoke inside you this power whenever you wish to help you stand against life's conflicts and obstacles. Spend some moments experiencing this energy.

Then, the veils fall away from you, and see Babalon standing over you, wearing a sheath-like garment similar to those worn by Ancient Egyptian women. You rise to kneel before her. Babalon takes a cup from the altar and hands this to you, bidding you to drink from it. When you taste the liquid within, you find it is red wine, but you sense there might be something more in it. But that is a secret you will never discover. You drink from this cup with the knowledge that it contains Babalon's essence. Then you hand the cup back to her. You stand up and for a moment gaze into those deep, mysterious eyes. Then you leave the tower.

If you wish to approach Babalon from a female perspective, the pathworking begins the same way. You enter the tower and find a group of people waiting for Babalon to appear in her temple. But at the moment when the lamps go out, you find yourself pulled into the body of the goddess. When the light comes back, you are Babalon, sitting upon the golden throne, and the people in the room bow down to you.

You wear the ceremonial costume of Babalon, adorned with floating veils, over a simple white shift. Your feet are bare, and you wear around your neck a pendant of a seven-pointed star. You hold a white serpent in each hand. They writhe in your hold, but you control them. You are filled with their power, their essence. As long as you hold them, their energy pours into you.

Now you rise from the throne and bend down to release the serpents. They form a circle and then disperse.

A prone figure lies upon the floor in the centre of the

room. The rest of the group kneel in a circle around you. You begin to dance, aware of everyone's attention upon you, which feeds you as much as the serpents did before. You feel powerful and beautiful. You feel free and graceful. The dance is sacred and empowering. You dance around the prone figure and begin to shed your veils over them, until you are dressed only in the shift.

The person on the floor kneels before you, in awe of you. You know they seek your power, are starving for it. This power is limitless and cannot be drained. You give it willingly and offer the cup. From you comes life, as you are the Great Mother, and new life is not simply reproduction of the species. As the person who drinks is empowered, so your own power is enriched. You become aware that even when you return to normal consciousness, this power of Babalon will remain within you. You can call upon it at any time.

When you are ready to leave the pathworking, go back to sit upon the throne.

Return to the garden by visualising the central tree clearly. This is your beacon and your guide. Be aware that a part of yourself remained there while you were travelling. It was and is your anchor. Return to that part of yourself simply by thinking this. You find yourself standing beneath the tree, feeling calm and refreshed. Return to normal consciousness and open your eyes.

Goddesses of War and Battlegrounds

Based upon a vintage illustration

Fierce Sisters

Originally, goddesses of the battlegrounds had specific functions, such as gathering up the souls of the dead and transporting them to the afterlife, whatever form that took in their particular tradition. They might also have been called upon by priests or priestesses in the service of kings to reveal the outcomes of conflict – who would live and who would die. Who would win. Occasionally, they might take up arms themselves and fight for those who most revered them, or – as in the case of Athene in the Trojan War – to enact revenge on someone who'd offended them.

Nowadays, people rely on governments, politics and, if all else fails, armies to protect them from hostile invaders. Conflicts are no longer resolved by two armies throwing themselves at each other from opposite ends of an open space, in a chaos of flailing limbs and weapons and the screams of horses. In our time, weapons can deliver their devastation from afar.

The old goddesses are no longer called upon to wander the battlefields, collecting lost souls from the dead and dying. Nor are they summoned to predict outcomes – our leaders have logarithms for such things in the 21st century. But where these fierce females do remain relevant is in bestowing upon us the strength and courage of a warrior, when we are faced with life's minor battles.

When we have to stand up to bullies or fight for a cause we believe is for the greater good, or defend someone weaker and more vulnerable than ourselves, then who better to call upon than ferocious female archetypes like Andraste or Scáthach, who will fill us with fire and valour, and the belief we can win.

Statue of Boudicca and her Daughters in London

Andraste
Goddess of the Iceni Queen

'Let us, therefore, go against the Romans, trusting boldly to good fortune. Let us show them that they are hares and foxes trying to rule over dogs and wolves.'

When Boudicca had finished speaking, she employed a type of divination, letting a hare escape from the fold of her dress; and since it ran on what they considered the auspicious side, the whole multitude shouted with pleasure, and Boudicca, raising her hand toward heaven, said: 'I thank you, Andraste, and call upon you as woman speaking to woman ... I beg you for victory and preservation of liberty.'

Adapted from a passage by Cassius Dio

Andraste is remembered mainly as being the goddess upon whom the ancient Celtic queen Boudicca called for aid, in her war against the Romans in England. Boudicca, also known in a Latinised form of her name as Boadicea, was ruler of the Iceni tribe and fought against Roman occupation in AD 60/61. She was initially married to King Prasutagus, who was an ally of Rome, and had managed to retain some independence for his people. When he died, Prasutagus left his estate jointly to his daughters and the Roman emperor, supposedly in the belief this would afford some protection for his family. However, it would appear the opposite was true. Although no clear facts remain as to why his will was ignored, the outcome was that – according to the Roman historian Tacitus – his kingdom was pillaged, his wife whipped, and his daughters raped. Another explanation for Boudicca's dispute with the Romans was given by Cassius Dio, who claimed Boudicca's decision to revolt was connected with loans that had been made to Prasutagus, which were all called in at once. Either or both of these accounts might have some validity. Whatever the truth of the matter, Boudicca was incensed, and willing to put her life at risk to take revenge. While she had some impressive victories against the Roman legions, she was eventually defeated and died shortly afterwards.

Facts concerning this ancient queen are scant, partly because she was largely ignored as a historical figure for centuries, until the Victorians took an interest in her and revived her as an important person in British history. Boudicca's name was thought most likely to stem from a Celtic word meaning 'victory' or 'victorious'. Similarities were then perceived between her and Queen Victoria. Andraste, the Celtic queen's patron goddess, is regarded as a symbol of victory and strength, a goddess of war, battlefields and ravens (carrion birds who devour the dead).

The majority of stories about Boudicca are most likely folklore rather than accurate historical accounts. There are no written records of her committing atrocities or sacrificing captives of war, but as she amassed a huge mob of followers, it's possible some of these people may be responsible for acts credited to Boudicca herself. It's said, for example, that she never took captives but killed all her enemies, sometimes sacrificing them to Andraste in a sacred grove. Tacitus describes how after Boudicca sacked Londinium, the Iceni and their allies captured all the Roman women, took them to a grove dedicated to the war goddess and here executed them. The details are grisly; the account describes how the breasts of the women's corpses were cut off and forced into their mouths, and thereafter they were impaled on poles. If this actually happened, it's a hideous mutilation of the dead and a grim blood sacrifice. But whether this story is true or not has been lost to the mists of time. Propaganda has existed throughout history, and Tacitus was firmly on the side of the Romans.

Another story suggests that the hare is a sacred animal of Andraste, but again this isn't a known fact but largely a supposition. According to Cassius Dio, Boudicca released a hare she'd concealed in her robes before her last battle, perhaps as a form of divination that was popular in those times: the direction in which the hare ran would denote the most auspicious position for her army to take. But over time, the hare has simply been absorbed as a symbol of Andraste. Some stories now say that Boudicca released the hare to seek the favour of the goddess, or for her sacred creature to run first into battle. Boudicca called upon Andraste as a 'sister' at this time, so was perhaps a priestess of the goddess.

Modern pagans have connected Andraste with a variety of goddesses – the deities of the Romano-Celtic period are numerous, so this isn't surprising. As with many other deities of ancient history, Romano-Celtic goddesses would have had local variants, which would often have included different names. There were several warrior goddesses, who rode in chariots, for example. Communication between settlements would have been limited in comparison to what we experience today. A goddess's name and nature could change dramatically, as her aspects were spoken of upon a long and winding road. If only half the legends are true, perhaps Andraste *was* propitiated by blood sacrifice. We might never know. However, if surviving accounts are to be believed, Boudicca almost certainly called upon Andraste for victory in battle. But, as with so many ancient goddesses who are now revered in modern times, it's not so much the truth of lost history that's important as how the goddess has evolved. We can be sure that the way people interact with her now is very different to how the Iceni venerated her.

The goddess is said to have had a more benign, lunar aspect as Andred, a deity of love and fertility, but whether these two goddesses were in fact connected, or that connection has been affixed by modern practitioners can't be confirmed for certain. But this doesn't matter. Andraste has her modern incarnation, a strong, fierce goddess to call upon for strength and victory, but who acts from a position of protection and nurturing – a lioness who is fiercely protective, rather than cruel and bloodthirsty.

Meeting Andraste

Begin the pathworking by entering the Garden of Gateways. To meet with Andraste, you will go into the eastern part of the garden.

Take the appropriate exit from the centre and follow the path to the east.

Once you pass through the gateway, you find yourself on the track that leads to the crossroads and the rising sun. You are in a landscape of heathland with occasional groves of trees. The land is wild and windy. Birds of prey ride on the winds above you, their enormous wings spread wide. They utter screeching cries.

You notice that there are many hares darting through the thickets and heather. They seem to be unnaturally large and appear very powerful. You know these are creatures associated with Andraste and also with divination. Perhaps they'll have a message for you.

You see the cross-roads just ahead, and as you draw close to it, you hear a strange, thundering noise. Presently, you realise this heralds the approach of a chariot drawn by two large and powerful horses. The chariot careens towards you, as if driven by a lunatic. As it draws close, you see that the wheels are spiked with long blades, designed to slice the legs of enemies.

You can see now that the chariot is driven by a woman. She looks extremely fierce, with a mass of bright red hair that flies out behind her. Powerfully built, she wears leather armour over a woollen robe, with a long cloak around her shoulders, which appears to be fashioned from hare skins.

The warrior woman pulls her horses, which you realise are mares, to a prancing halt at the end of the crossroads. At this moment, all the hares around you stand up on their hind legs and stare madly at the woman, their long ears erect. She pulls from her cloak the largest hare you've ever seen. It looks vicious, its lips pulled back from its sharp front teeth in a snarl. Its legs kick as it tries to escape the woman's hold. She holds it up by the ears for a moment and calls out some words you can't understand. Then, she releases the animal and it leaps away from her, somersaulting in the air. All the other hares run away swiftly, as if in terror.

The large hare disappears into a copse of trees near the track. The warrior woman in the chariot, yelling at you in an unknown language and gesturing wildly, clearly indicates you should follow the animal.

Obeying this instruction, you go to the copse and enter it. The trees in there are old, gnarled hawthorns that huddle together like hags of sticks and leaves. The centre of the copse is a clearing, and you can see the remains of old fires there. There are poles around the edge of this space, which are adorned with human skulls. Clearly, this is a place of power and of significance to those who revere Andraste.

The hare has come to a halt in the middle of the clearing and now stands up on its hind legs, staring at you. You return the stare without fear. The animal stamps its hind legs and transforms into a woman. You realise this is Andraste. She's very tall and, like the warrior woman who summoned her, appears strong and fierce. She too wears a cloak of hare skins, which drapes around her towering form. It's decorated with the paws, ears and heads of the animals. Her hair is thick and fair, wound and plaited with hare bones. Her expression is haughty. Andraste is the goddess of victory in battle. She admires strength but scorns weakness. Her attitude is not exactly welcoming, but she appears prepared to tolerate your presence and will listen to you.

Now, you can ask for her aid with victory in your own life. You desire her influence, so you may succeed in all ventures where you feel you will face opposition. This doesn't necessarily mean obstructions caused by other people, but also unavoidable circumstances and coincidence. You ask for Andraste to 'even up the game' in all your endeavours, so that you have a fighting chance of victory and may achieve your goals.

Once you have finished communing with Andraste concerning your personal circumstances, you may ask her to reveal her mysteries. Tell her you wish to find out more about her cult and her connections with Boudicca and the Iceni tribe, and the other tribes and clans of Ancient Europe.

After you have finished your conversation, Andraste turns back into a hare and runs from the ancient grove. By the time you reach the outside of the clearing, you can see the hare has returned to the chariot of the warrior woman, who turns her vehicle back towards the dawn and rides out of sight.

In the distance, you can see the rising sun above the road. It is time for you to return to the garden.

Return to the garden by visualising the central tree clearly. This is your beacon and your guide. Be aware that a part of yourself remained there while you were travelling. It was and is your anchor. Return to that part of yourself simply by thinking this. You find yourself standing beneath the tree, feeling calm and refreshed. Return to normal consciousness and open your eyes.

The Morrígan by Danielle Lainton

The Morrígan
Walker of the Battlefields

*'Over his head is shrieking
A lean hag, quickly hopping
Over the points of their weapons and shields –
She is the grey-haired Morrigu.'*

From an ancient Irish manuscript

Some goddesses of war might thunder in their chariots towards the enemy, but there are others who utter chilling predictions concerning the outcome of hostilities and who haunt the battlefield in the aftermath. While the crows circle and utter their harsh calls, clattering down to partake of a grisly feast, the Morrígan walks among the dead.

Unlike some of the goddesses in this book, there are a host of surviving stories about The Morrígan – enough to fill a book themselves. Recent archaeological evidence suggests her worship (or perhaps of a goddess – or goddesses – very much like her) extends back to 3000BC. She's a recurring figure in Irish myth – a supernatural female rather than an actual goddess – and many legends describe her appearing to kings and warriors and being instrumental in matters of fate and doom. Mainly, she is associated with war, particularly with prophesying death in battle. Should a warrior come across a strange woman washing his bloodied armour in a stream, he knows he won't survive a coming conflict.

The Morrígan has different aspects but is generally encountered as a crone – or a beautiful young woman who can transform into a crone. She is also a shapeshifter, who can be a crow, a wolf, an eel and a cow – among other forms. She was strongly connected with carrion birds, particularly the crow, and was said to fly above battlefields while conflict was in progress. These transformations are all described in ancient Irish legends. In her role of warrior goddess, she would occasionally take part in the fighting herself, but generally she was more inclined to prophesy the outcomes of war rather than lend a hand in them.

Some of the stories you'll find about her now are the products of reinterpretation with a modern gloss. Certain old myths mention her association with cows and sovereignty, but this doesn't suggest a nurturing mother goddess, as some writers believe. Cows meant wealth, and sovereignty was a matter of great importance to those who held power. It's claimed by some that The Morrígan's association with war is a later addition, and that in her earliest forms she was a nature and fertility goddess, associated with birth. While some very ancient artefacts have been found across Europe, depicting more 'earth motherly' goddesses with crowlike attributes, they don't necessarily depict the Irish Morrígan. However, as she could be interpreted as representing the circle of life, we found it appropriate to link her aspect of death with this continual cycle, particularly with rebirth. This is reflected in the pathworking that follows.

Another interpretation proposes that The Morrígan is the dark sorceress Morgan le Fay from Arthurian legend, but as the stories of King Arthur mentioning this character are a much later fictional romance, (written by Thomas Malory in the 15th Century), this is unlikely. However, because this notion has become popular among some writers and practitioners, we could say the Morrígan has now absorbed it into her composition.

She's also said to have a triple aspect, as in the Maiden, Mother and Crone found throughout pagan belief. In Irish myth, she did have two sisters, or sometimes the three goddesses were grouped together, when they were known collectively as The Morrígan. Modern writers and scholars don't always agree on who these sisters were. The set of names varies. In one version, the Morrígan are Badb, Macha and Nemain; in another they are Badb, Macha and Anand. So she can be three goddesses or one.

There's also dispute over what The Morrígan's name means, but all of the interpretations are fascinating. The first part of the name 'Mor' could derive from an Old English word 'maere', which meant terror or something monstrous. This word also gave rise to the term 'nightmare' – 'night terror'. The 'rigan' part of the name can be translated as 'queen'. Some scholars interpret the name as 'phantom queen', but perhaps 'terrifying queen' is more accurate. The name can also change meaning depending upon the accents placed over certain letters. If it is spelled Mórrígan, it means 'great queen'. Those who've attempted to link the Morrígan to Morgan le Fay, (who is mentioned in ancient Welsh literature), think that the name is connected to the sea, as 'Mor' is similar to môr, the Welsh word for sea. However, there are no other sources that link this battlefield goddess to the ocean.

There are many colourful tales of the Morrígan in Irish myth, and here is an example, which illustrates several of her aspects. The story goes that the hero of Ulster, Cú Chulainn, was engaged in a series of conflicts with the enemy queen of Connacht, who was named Medb. The queen wished to steal a prize bull belonging to the people of Ulster. When the fighting-men of Ulster were disabled by a curse, Cú Chulainn defended his people's territory – and property – alone, by defeating Medb's champions one by one in single combat at various fords – a process that had lasted many months.

Just before one of these legendary fights, a beautiful young woman appears to Cú Chulainn. She offers him both her love and her aid in the fight to come, but the hero rejects her advances. He has no idea that the woman he has spurned is the Morrígan herself, but she then reveals her true nature to him and also makes it clear, no doubt, she's not happy with his response. During the following combat, the slighted Morrígan attempts to foul Cú Chulainn's chances. First, she turns into an eel, and tries to trip him in the water of the ford, but he breaks her ribs. Next, she turns into a wolf, and in this form stampedes cattle across the ford, but Cú Chulainn puts out one of her eyes with a sling-shot. Then, swiftly, she transforms into a white, red-eared heifer, who is leading the stampede of cattle. But again, Cú Chulainn foils her by breaking one of her legs with his sling-shot. He then goes on to defeat his enemy.

After the fight, the Morrígan appears once more to him, this time in the form of an old woman milking a cow. She bears the three injuries he inflicted upon her in her animal forms. The hero accepts three drinks of milk from her, and with each drink, he blesses her, which causes her injuries to heal. Only a fool wouldn't make amends to such a powerful creature. It was said that Cú Chulainn was amongst the most beautiful of men, so perhaps that's partly why she doesn't hold her grudge for long. It's interesting to note that in her cow form she is white with red ears – this colouration is found in other supernatural beasts, including the hounds that run with the Wild Hunt.

Meeting The Morrígan

Begin the pathworking by entering the Garden of Gateways. To meet with the Morrígan, you will go into the western part of the garden. You are seeking, in this visit, the aspect of the west pertaining to sunset and autumn.

Take the appropriate exit from the centre and follow the path to the west, which leads to the setting sun.

You emerge from the garden into a forested, mountainous area. The sun is setting on a late autumn day, around the time of Samhain, known also as Halloween.

You are at the base of a hill, which is covered in tall pines and other evergreens. The sinking sun casts ruby rays through the trunks of the pines, and the scene, while stark, is quite beautiful. You can hear the occasional call of rooks high in the trees and the air is full of the scent of pine and earth. The ground between the trees is covered in old brown pine needles, but sometimes there is a splash of greenery in the form of ferns and other forest plants.

A path leads up the hill between the trees and you follow it. As you climb the gradually steepening path, you become more aware of the cries of the birds. At first, you could only hear sporadic caws, as if from a few crows or rooks, but now it seems a host of birds are gathering. You recognise the cries of ravens too. As you climb upwards, the cries become a cacophony in the trees around you, getting louder and louder. You realise the birds are returning to their nests at twilight, high and unseen in the trees.

Eventually, the hill begins to even out, and you realise you've reached the summit. By now, the cries of the birds are deafening. They throng in the trees at the crown of the hill.

On the path in front of you, a dark figure appears, draped in a long black cloak. As you walk towards it, you see it's a haglike woman, whose enveloping cloak is fashioned entirely of black feathers. Beneath it, she wears a tattered dark robe. Her head is adorned with a hood, which is also covered in iridescent black feathers, as well as a long, wooden beak that covers the upper part of her face. This is the Morrígan. She is the embodiment of the carrion birds, who pick at remains on the fields of battle. She is also the embodiment of excarnation, the practice in which the dead are not buried or burned but left out for wild animals and birds to eat.

You can see that behind the Morrígan, in a clearing, are high wooden platforms, bearing the remains of human carcases. A flock of black carrion birds is pecking at them.

The Morrígan stands motionless before you, both hands gripping a long, carved staff, upon which she leans. It's wound with rags and feathers and is tipped by the skull of a carrion bird. You are compelled to gaze into her eyes, and it seems as if you're being drawn right into them, to view the world as she does.

Suddenly, you find that you have been taken up into the sky. You have transformed into a great crow and are part of a flock of carrion birds of several different types. You are wheeling around the sky, and below you a chaotic, fierce battle is taking place. The ground is slick with blood and mud. Soldiers are maimed and cut down. Some are dying from fatal wounds. Others are already dead. The ground is covered with bodies and severed limbs. As you hover over this site, you see that birds are already feasting on the bodies at the edge of the field, where some warriors have crawled to die or been flung there.

You become aware that the spirits of slain warriors are rising up from the dead bodies. The birds encourage the spirits to rise and then accompany them. They head towards a funnel of light high above. You fly upwards to draw closer to this phenomenon, until suddenly you are within it. Everything is white. You can see no imagery at all at first, then start to glimpse the first images of the afterlife, knowing that this is one of the Morrígan's purposes. She oversees the transition of the souls of those killed in battle, from the world of the living to the world of the dead; heaven, Valhalla. You know you are here only as a witness, borrowing the form of a guide for the dead. It is not your time to pass through to the next world and then on to rebirth.

Now, you pass through the light, and as you do so, you hear the cry of a new born child. You become aware of a new environment and find yourself in a log cabin. Here, you see a woman in the throes of giving birth, attended by a mid-wife, who is dressed in a cloak of feathers. You realise this too is the Morrígan, and that she is not simply connected with death but also rebirth, the whole round of life.

Her work done, the mid-wife leaves the cabin and you follow her. Now spend some time in her company and see if she has any messages or tasks for you.

When you are ready, return to normal consciousness.

Return to the garden by visualising the central tree clearly. This is your beacon and your guide. Be aware that a part of yourself remained there while you were travelling. It was and is your anchor. Return to that part of yourself simply by thinking this. You find yourself standing beneath the tree, feeling calm and refreshed. Return to normal consciousness and open your eyes.

Pakhet by Storm Constantine

Pakhet
Huntress of the Red Desert

O You of the dawn who wake and sleep,
O You who are in limpness, dwelling aforetime in Nedit,
I have appeared as Pakhet the Great,
whose eyes are keen and whose claws are sharp,
the lioness who sees and catches by night....

From the Ancient Egyptian *Coffin Texts*,
translated by Raymond O. Faulkner

The fierce Egyptian goddess Sekhmet has been written about extensively in modern pagan literature, and her veneration is common among practitioners. But there is another lioness-headed deity, who was very similar to Sekhmet, and who was a patron goddess of the female pharaoh Hatshepsut. This was Pakhet (Pah-*ket*). Her name means 'she who scratches', and had spelling variants in Pachet, Pehket, Pashtet and Pasht. Her main attribute was as a goddess of war.

Pakhet shares attributes and epithets with other feline- and leonine-headed goddesses (including Bast and Tefnut, as well as Sekhmet.) She, like them, was associated with the sun, so is generally shown in ancient art as wearing a sun disk as part of her headdress. One of her titles was 'Goddess of the Mouth of the Wadi', which is shared by Sekhmet. A wadi is a desert waterway or channel that is dry except during the rainy season. Another title connected with water is 'She Who Opens the Ways of the Stormy Rains'. Wadis tend to be replenished by flash floods caused by storms, and the people believed a goddess had to be responsible.

Pakhet protected against vermin and dangerous creatures, and could be invoked as a ferocious warrior, but she also had the epithet of 'Night Huntress', and in this form – perhaps in the shape of a caracal or desert-lynx – she stalked alone in the night, hunting through the desert for prey. It can be assumed, then, she could be invoked in this way – to hunt down predators or enemies. Pakhet was also associated with desert storms.

Like Bast, she had a 'mother goddess' aspect, and protected mothers and children – several of the feline and leonine goddesses appear to have had this role, presumably because of the way female cats and lionesses cared for their young.

But what sets Pakhet apart from the other feline/leonine goddesses is her connection to the female pharaoh Hatshepsut. The pharaoh commissioned a vast underground temple to Pakhet near an area now known as el Minya. Hatshepsut and her daughters built other temples to Pakhet, many of which have been destroyed or were defaced by later pharaohs and foreign invaders.

The Greeks, however, who arrived in Egypt after Hatshepsut's time, appropriated the el Minya site and named it Speos Artemidos. This is because they saw in Pakhet similarities to their own huntress goddess, Artemis. The name of the site meant 'Cave of Artemis'. An abundance of mummified cats has been found in the temple catacombs, which have been excavated extensively. These animals were probably slain ceremonially on site and given as offerings to the goddess, or else killed to act as messengers, carrying petitions for favour to Pakhet's ears. This type of sacrifice was also a common practice in connection with the cat-headed Bast. Mummified hawks have also been found at the site, suggesting a connection with the god Horus: sometimes Pakhet was referred to as Pakhet-Horus. Some writers think this means she was believed, at least in that part of Egypt, to be associated with the mother of Horus, which in some areas was believed to be Hathor. Pakhet was also sometimes known as Pakhet-Weret-Hekau. The second and third words of the name mean 'Great in Magic', which was an epithet applied to Isis and Hathor too. Goddesses were often mingled and tangled in Egyptian mythology – the stories that remain don't have the most clear-cut narratives found in traditions such as Norse, Celtic and Greek.

Meeting Pakhet

Begin the pathworking by entering the Garden of Gateways. To meet with Pakhet, you will go into the southern part of the garden, seeking the aspect of fire and a hot desert land.

Take the appropriate exit from the centre and follow the path to the south, which leads to the summer sun.

You find yourself in a vast desert landscape, just as the sun begins to sink down the sky in the late afternoon. This is the ancient land of Khem, which is an old name for Egypt. There are dry, craggy, pale mountains around you. Go west into the desert, and as you do so, dusk creeps in and night begins to fall around you.

At first you are alone, then you're aware that you are possibly being stalked by a wild animal. The closer it comes, the more you realise it's a large feline, but you can't see it clearly. Yet it does not attack.

You come to an opening in the ground and see below you a stairway that leads down to a structure that looks like the entrance to a tomb. As you go down, you pass through a portal, whose lintel is decorated with a winged scarab beetle. Beyond, you enter a chamber that's lit by oil lamps on poles. The chamber is large and square. In front of you is a pit and within it are fierce female lynxes that are clearly responding to your presence. You feel they would attack if they had a chance.

Beyond the pit there is a raised set of steps and standing at the top of the steps, almost like a statue, is a woman dressed in golden garments but with the head of a desert lynx. This is Pakhet: she is not a statue but a living creature. She stands in a pharaonic posture, carrying the artefacts of sovereignty, the crook and the flail. She wears a pleated, red linen gown, with a wide gold pectoral decoration around the neck and upper chest.

Having made your way around the edge of the pit, you stand in front of her, maybe ten feet away, at the top of the steps. She doesn't move or speak, and you wonder whether she is really a statue.

You gaze into her eyes and feel as if you're swallowed by them. You become Pakhet and look through her eyes.

Now you are out in the desert and realise you've become the large cat you sensed stalking you earlier on. Your senses are enhanced. You can see clearly in the darkness and your nose can detect myriad scents a human nose could not pick up. You slink through the shadows thrown by sharp rocks, keeping pace with the person – who is also you – who now approaches the underground temple from which you came.

You know now that the cat who followed you was the goddess herself, and that she was not stalking you but protecting you from other predators as you travelled through the desert. She was also alert to shield you from any other influences that might have wished to do you harm.

When you are ready, release your connection to the lynx, so that you once more stand before Pakhet in her underground shrine. Ask her to protect you whenever you have to pass through the deserts of life. This can mean many things, such as loneliness, threat, illness or deprivation. Pakhet will be there for you and will protect and guide you.

Thank Pakhet for her protection and leave the temple the way you came. Now the lynxes in the pit are at ease when you pass them; they barely take any notice of you.

Go back into the desert and once again be aware of the presence of the protective influence of Pakhet. Walk a short way with her until you're ready to end the pathworking.

Return to the garden by visualising the central tree clearly. This is your beacon and your guide. Be aware that a part of yourself remained there while you were travelling. It was and is your anchor. Return to that part of yourself simply by thinking this. You find yourself standing beneath the tree, feeling calm and refreshed. Return to normal consciousness and open your eyes.

Scáthach by Danielle Lainton

Scáthach
Queen of the Proving Grounds

When you are a peerless champion,
great extremity awaits you,
alone against the vast herd.
Warriors will be set aside against you,
necks will be broken by you,
your sword will strike strokes to the rear
against Sétanta's gory stream.

From the ancient Irish poem *Verba Scathaige*
Describing Scáthach's divination for Cú Chulainn

Scáthach (pronounced roughly **Ska**-hath) was a Scottish warrior queen, although the stories about her derive from Irish mythology. She was said to have trained the Ulster hero Cú Chulainn in the arts of warfare. Variants of her name include Sgathaich, and the land of Scotland in these myths was known as Alpae or Alpeach.

Scáthach lived upon the Isle of Skye, the largest island of the Inner Hebrides off Scotland. Its ancient name in Gaelic was either An t-Eilean Sgitheanach or Eilean a' Cheò, or Skíð in Norse. In the meditation we'll refer to the island as Sgitheanach (pronounced, roughly: **Skee**-an-och). The actual meaning of the name is unclear.

The warrior queen resided in a fortress named Dún Scáith (or Dún Sgathaich), which meant 'Castle of Shadows', pronounced roughly Dun Skar. There are ruins on Skye – Dun Sgathaich near Tarskavaig – that date back to the twelfth century, and these are believed to stand upon the site of Dún Scáith.

Scáthach was the daughter of Árd-Greimne, the Lord of Lethra. She had a sister named Aífe (or Aiofe) and there was great rivalry between them. In the original stories, Scáthach was a fierce heroine, rather than a goddess, and was described as 'The Shadowy One' or 'The Warrior Maid'.

Many young warriors wanted to train with the legendary Scáthach but had to pass tests to earn that honour. She set up defences around her castle that were difficult and dangerous to penetrate and would only take on trainees who were able to make their way safely to her. Many died in the attempt. A couple of the obstacles are described as the 'Plain of Ill-Fortune' and the 'Glen of Peril'. Anyone seeking Scáthach also had to negotiate the 'Bridge of Leaping', which, when anyone set foot on it, flipped up and hurled them back to where they'd come from. Successful candidates were trained in a variety of disciplines, including pole-vaulting, (presumably to help breach castle walls), and underwater combat.

As mentioned earlier, one of Scáthach's students was the fabled Cú Chulainn. Seeking the best warrior training possible, Cú Chulainn travelled to Skye with a friend (or sometimes two friends, according to different versions of the tale). After completing his training, Scáthach awarded him with an exceptional barbed spear, or harpoon, of her own design, named the Gáe Bulg. Its first strike was said always to be fatal.

The story continues, telling us that Cú Chulainn aided Scáthach to protect her domain. Her sister Aífe had set herself up as a rival queen or chieftain, but Cú Chulainn helped Scáthach to defeat her, and Aífe was obliged to make peace with her sister. The Ulster hero clearly had a great impact on the family in other ways. He was said to have fathered a child with Aífe, and after that slept with Scáthach's daughter, Uathach. He ended up duelling with Uathach's lover Cochar Croibhe, and killed him, but this fight didn't arise from Uathach's infidelity. It's said that

Uathach would often spar with Cú Chulainn, and once during combat practice, Cú Chulainn accidentally broke her fingers. Her lover heard her screams, and in fury challenged Cú Chulainn to the duel in which he lost his life. Cú Chulainn was said to be full of remorse for this and pledged himself to serving Uathach thereafter – presumably for a limited time.

The old stories relate that once Cú Chulainn's warrior training was complete, Scáthach also rewarded him by taking him to her bed.

Scáthach appears to have been a free woman, who had no husband. She did, however, have several children, according to different stories. As well as Uathach, there were the sons Cet and Cuar who were trained – presumably as warriors – within a magical yew tree. There were also other daughters (in some accounts listed as Lasair, Ingean Bhuidhe, and Latiaran), but Uathach seems to have been the most influential. She eventually trained young warriors with her mother and guarded the entrance to Dún Scáith.

In some stories, Scáthach is described as having the gift of prophecy and being skilled with divination, in particular palmistry, known as *imbas forosnai*. She allegedly divined for Cú Chulainn and foresaw many of his battles.

In other old tales, she was said to have eventually become the Celtic goddess of the dead, leading those slain in battle to Tír na nÓg (a Celtic vision of the Land of Eternal Youth). But it's only in recent times that she's become truly 'deified' – as has occurred with many other figures from old legend cycles, such as Cerridwen. But again, if goddesses arise from myths because modern pagans invest them with this role, then it is valid. The characters take on the attributes given to them and become powerful symbols and god-forms in their own right.

The pronunciations provided for words included in the meditation are only approximate. You can visit the website https://forvo.com and search the Gaelic section for clear and more precise pronunciations.

Meeting Scáthach

Begin the pathworking by entering the Garden of Gateways. To meet with Scáthach, you will go into the northern part of the garden. Here you are seeking the element of earth, the rugged landscape of Scotland, the solid power of the mountains.

Take the appropriate exit from the centre of the garden and follow the path to the cave in the north. As soon as you cross the threshold of the first chamber, the air grows moist and you're aware of a faint scent of the ocean. You pass quickly through the cave and along a straight passageway, to emerge into a new landscape.

You're standing on a clifftop pathway above a restless northern sea, beneath a blue summer sky, roiling with fast-moving clouds. Below you lies a small village of primitive buildings, above a deep harbour. Here a ship is moored, which you know is your destination.

You walk down to the village and board the ship, whose crew regard you warily. The ship will take you to the island of Sgitheanach where the famous warrior queen Scáthach resides. As you cross the dark, churning sea, you think about your intention for making this journey. You desire to be trained by Scáthach, in order to overcome physical limitations and be capable of facing any enemy victoriously. But Scáthach only agrees to train student warriors she considers worthy, and to win her approval you must undergo her trials – enter her proving grounds.

Eventually, the captain of your ship lowers a boat in which you must travel alone to the island. You climb down into this vessel and begin to row to shore. You see before you a rugged landscape, the shore comprising many peninsulas and bays, with deep green forests, hills and mountains in the background. It is so raw and beautiful beneath the dappled light of sunlight and clouds, it seems like the home of gods to you.

As you draw nearer, you see two tall women standing upon the shore, apparently waiting for you. Without words, they help you land the boat. They are dressed in leather armour – close fitting tunics and leggings – and their abundant brown hair is bound up. You know that these are two of the daughters of Scáthach, and they're aware of your purpose for coming to this place.

Commune for a few moments with these women. They might reveal their names to you. They talk to you about how the trials ahead represent people, situations and events in life. Whatever you face will be aspects of Scáthach's proving grounds. Through your training, you will learn how to face such situations courageously and to fight monsters if you have to – whatever form they may take. The hero warrior also fights for others.

The daughters give you a selection of equipment and weapons you'll need for the trials ahead, but these appear flimsy to you. However, the women seem aware of your doubt and tell you the greatest weapons and the most efficient tools, are your own courage and conviction. Eventually, you set off in the direction the daughters point out to you.

You arrive at a flat expanse of grassland, which you know must be the Plain of Ill-Fortune, the first of the trials. Sit down at the edge of this plain and contemplate what it means to you. Circumstances don't always go in the direction we want them to, and unwanted obstacles can emerge without warning. Gaze upon the plain and see what obstacles in your life are represented there, both from the past and the present, and perhaps also the future. Then, in your own way, confronting your own objects of ill-fortune, cross the plain.

Once you have completed this trial, you walk on, into a mountainous area. You come to a deep gorge that seems to extend endlessly before you in both directions. Around you is a forest of young trees. Across the gorge is what seems to be a safe, solid bridge. You set foot on it and walk forward tentatively. All seems well. Then, halfway across, the bridge flips up and you're flung high into the air, landing back where you came from. The gorge and its treacherous, deceiving bridge represent what seem to be insurmountable obstacles. Think about how this could represent aspects of your own life and circumstances. You can see no way to cross the gorge, but then you remember another trial from the legends – the Bridge of Leaping. You recall also how part of Scáthach's training involves pole-vaulting. Use what tools you have and your own imagination to overcome this trial. Consider how this kind of thinking might be applied to situations in reality.

On the other side of the gorge, you move on and arrive eventually at a mouth of a deep, dark valley covered in brooding woodland. This, you realise, is the Glen of Peril. Strange noises issue from amid the trees. Dusk creeps over the land and serpentine mist coils around the roots of the ancient trees. You draw one of the weapons the daughters of Scáthach gave to you – but will this be enough with which to defend yourself? Perhaps you need fire also. What else is in your pack that will help?

Venture into the woodland and face the creatures and events that wait for you there. Not everything you encounter will be hostile, or it might appear so but then reveal itself as something else, something unexpected. A monster becomes an ally. An ally becomes a monster. A seemingly safe terrain turns savage. A wild terrain serves to defend you. Use whatever tools you can find to help you – whether they've been given to you by the daughters or else found in the landscape itself. You must stay in this place until dawn.

Once dawn arrives, you make your way out of the forest and emerge into an area of low hills. You think about the lessons of the night. On the skyline you see a mighty fortress and know that it is Dún Scáith, Scáthach's castle. A troupe of riders are coming towards you and, as they draw closer, you see they are led by Scáthach herself, dressed in her finest leather armour, which is highly polished and scored with curling symbols. She declares you have proven yourself in the trials and she will accept you as a student. She gives to you a spear as a token of her esteem. This is a beautiful object in comparison with the rough equipment you've had to work with throughout the proving grounds. The spear represents your determination, skill and ingenuity when facing the trials of life. From this moment on, you are stronger and wiser.

Now, having earned it, spend some time on the island in the company of Scáthach and her sons and daughters, celebrating your victory and planning your future. You may return to this island at any time in order to commune with Scáthach and train with her.

When you are ready to depart, return to the garden by visualising the central tree clearly. This is your beacon and your guide. Be aware that a part of yourself remained there while you were travelling. It was and is your anchor. Return to that part of yourself simply by thinking this. You find yourself standing beneath the tree, feeling calm and refreshed. Return to normal consciousness and open your eyes.

Scáthach's Realm by Storm Constantine

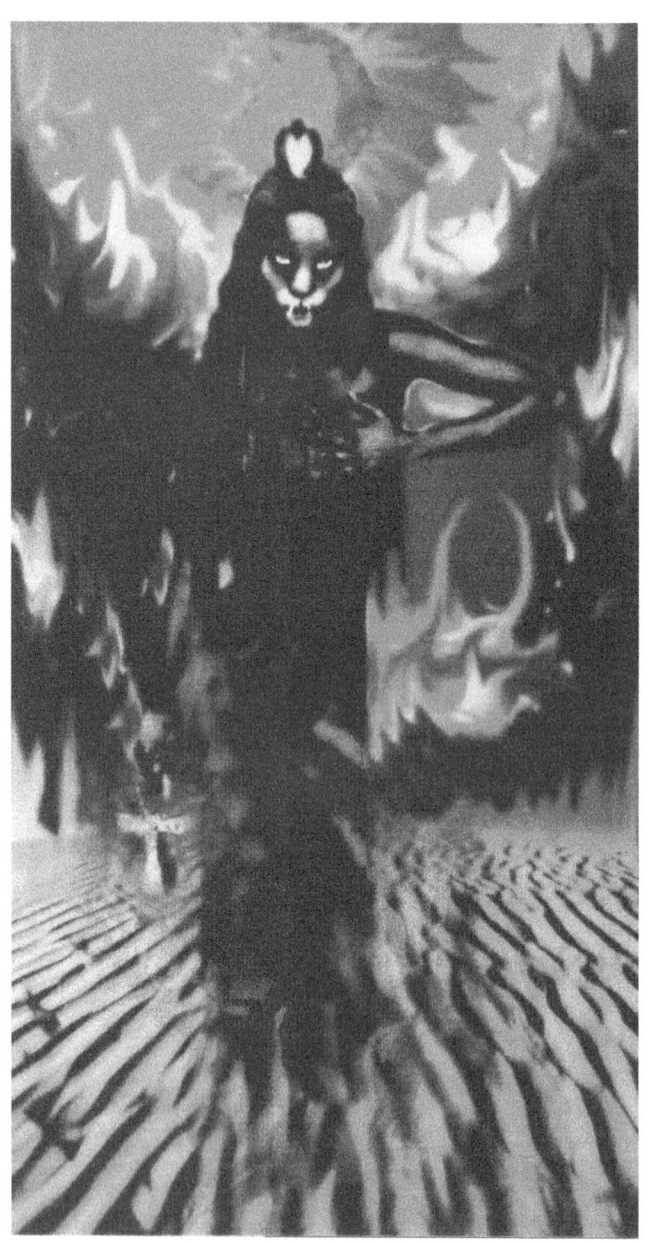

Sekhmet by Ruby

Sekhmet
Eye of Ra

Maggie Jennings

Oh Star of the Lion's Heart, I behold thee
Embolden my heart, oh Sekhmet,
Embolden my soul, Oh Flame, Oh Lion Star.

From 'Under Regulus' by Elizabeth St George

Sekhmet is an Egyptian goddess of bloodshed and war. She is lioness-headed, beautiful and very powerful, terrible and destructive. She was known as an Eye of Ra, since she represented the fiery power of the sun that did the bidding of Ra, the sun god – in particular smiting his enemies. This is the legend of how she was created:

And it came to pass when Ra, who came into being by himself, had established his kingship over men and gods together. Then mankind planned evil thoughts against Ra. Now as to His Majesty (life, prosperity and health!), he had become old... And his Majesty discerned the thoughts that were planned against him by mankind. And his Majesty (life, prosperity and health!) said to the gods who were among his following: 'Come, fetch for me my Eye, and also Shu, Tefnut and Geb... together with my god Nun, who shall bring his courtiers with him. Thou shalt bring them cautiously; let not mankind see, let not their hearts be awakened! Thou shalt come with them to the Great Palace, that they may give me their counsel, as they have done since

the time when I came forth from Nun...'
Then Ra said to Nun:
'O thou Eldest God, in whom I came into being, and ye Primeval Gods! Behold mankind, who came into being from my Eye! They have planned evil thoughts against me. Tell me what you would do about it! Behold I am seeking a solution and am not slaying them until I hear your opinion.'
.. And they all said unto His Majesty:
'Let thine Eye go forth to smite for thee those who plan with evil. However, the Eye has not sufficient power within itself to smite them for thee. Let it go forth as [Sekhmet]'
And so, then, this goddess arrived, and she slew mankind upon the desert... This is how Sekhmet came into being.

From a tomb text inscribed in the 19th Dynasty

In the story, Sekhmet gets so carried away with her work that she has to be stopped by deception – the gods create a brew of beer and red ochre, which looks like blood, and they fill the fields with it. Sekhmet drinks her fill and becomes so intoxicated she cannot continue her slaughter.

This might make Sekhmet seem like a terrifying force, bloodthirsty and ruthless. However, it is important to remember that although Sekhmet is the goddess of destruction, to the Ancient Egyptians this destruction was positive – she removed the enemies of Ra.

Sekhmet is often represented holding an ankh – the key of life – and crowned with the disc of the life-giving sun. She represents the power we can wield ourselves, should circumstances demand it, to destroy that which is dangerous to us. Sometimes negotiation just isn't an option. For example, at a cellular level, infection has to be destroyed – you can't negotiate with a virus! Another example might be when we are bullied – bullies often back down when we stand up to them. The lesson Sekhmet teaches us is that we all have access to this powerful force that we can draw on when needed, even if should we ultimately choose not to use it. We should embrace this ability and own it, as this gives us confidence and removes the need for us to be violent or aggressive (except in dire need). Some people become physically violent or verbally aggressive simply to make themselves feel strong, which in the end only reveals their insecurity. This has nothing to do with physical strength – positive destruction only requires a strong spirit. We have the power to defeat evil – and we also need to know when to stop. Once victory has been achieved, once we have 'nuked' something that is unacceptable, we can rest as Sekhmet did (although not necessarily in a drunken stupor!).

Meeting Sekhmet
Maggie Jennings

Begin the pathworking by entering the Garden of Gateways. To meet with Sekhmet, you will go into the southern part of the garden, from where you will venture into the hot land of Khem.

It is a summer evening. The air smells sweet and the sky is slowly dimming with the setting sun. You see the apple tree in the centre of the garden. The leaves are fresh and green, and you might even see tiny apples just starting to form along its branches. You hear running water and look down at the stream at the foot of the tree. The scent of cool water reaches you, and you hear birdsong and the faint hum of bees. Be aware that part of your spirit will always remain by the apple tree, and you may return to it whenever you wish.

You turn to the south. This is where you will find the realm of the element of fire. You walk through the gap in the hedge and find yourself facing the blazing sun of noon day. The garden around you appears beautifully exotic, with lush fruit trees and richly-scented flowers. This gives you the sense of being in a land with a naturally hot climate.

Before you is the high fence of the garden and the wooden gate. You walk through, closing the gate carefully behind you.

You find yourself in a desert, hot and silent, with sandy, rocky hills and valleys stretching out in front of you. The landscape is dotted with a few trees, which are twisted and small, but their shadows are long and stretch out towards you like fingers.

Shading your eyes against the sun of the late afternoon, you see a small hill to your right, on top of which stand high walls, sand-coloured like the desert. You shade your eyes to see more clearly and notice a huge gateway in the centre of the wall in front of you, flanked by enormous statues on each side. You perceive that the statues are also of a sand-coloured stone and represent four huge seated pharaohs, two on each side. Above the doorway is a small statue set above the lintel – it is of a lion-headed goddess.

You decide to investigate further, and walk up to the hill, carefully making your way across the uneven ground.

As you walk closer you see the temple is partly ruined, its gate hanging open and some areas of the roof missing. The statues are damaged. You peer through the gate and see before you the large space of what used to be a courtyard. It has pillars down the sides, and even a few ancient pictures with hieroglyphs painted on the walls, although they are faded and flaking with age. The temple is completely silent and appears to be deserted.

At the far end of the courtyard you see another door, which appears to lead to an inner sanctum. You decide to enter and find yourself in a space that was originally roofed, although now the light of the sinking sun pools on the floor, falling through ragged gaps in the stonework above you. You feel quite claustrophobic as you are surrounded by large pillars, covered with faded hieroglyphs and paintings of the Egyptian Gods, like the ones in the courtyard.

You walk towards the far end of the room. On a stone dais in front of you is a large throne, carved in stone. You are drawn to sit upon it, so walk up the steps to the dais and sit down, where you are able to see clearly the whole chamber before you. Then, to your surprise, you see that all has changed. The temple appears as it was centuries ago – it is full of people. Beyond, the courtyard is noisy with visitors and in this quiet area where you sit, priests move gracefully around the chamber, lighting lamps. One of them comes towards you and bows – holding out to you an offering of food and drink. You accept the offering and bow your head in thanks. You are aware that all is well in this place – everyone is engaged in their allotted tasks, busy and happy. You realise you are the ruler here.

But then there is a disturbance at the other end of the room. The double doors burst open and some soldiers pour in. They have weapons, swords and clubs, and start attacking the priests and visitors in the courtyard, creating chaos and confusion. You hear screaming from outside as everyone tries to escape. Some priests try to defend themselves and attack the soldiers, but it is no use, and blood spills in this sacred place as victims fall, mortally wounded.

You begin to fill with an immense feeling of rage, which vibrates through every cell in your body, making you tremble with fury. This feeling builds until it bursts out of you as a tremendous roar of hatred and anger, a roar that is louder than anything you have ever heard. The whole building resonates with the sound, and it seems to penetrate the very walls.

The deafening roar that comes from your body fills you with amazement. How can you make so much sound? You can feel it filling every cell in your body. It feels wonderful to be making such a ground-shaking noise.

Take a moment to revel in your power and majesty. You feel a sense of supreme energy and know that no-one or nothing can stand against you.

After a few moments, you realise that all the soldiers have gone, driven away by your terrifying roar. The people start returning to the courtyard, and some of them come into the inner sanctum to help the wounded, wash away the blood, and set everything in order once more. All is as it should be, and everyone is calm once more.

You decide to explore the temple further. You get up and see a small door behind the throne you've not noticed before. No-one takes any notice as you quickly slip through the door.

Now you find yourself in a lovely inner courtyard, open to the sky. There is a fountain in the centre and a little pool, surrounded with green plants. The sound of running water attracts you, so you go to the pool, intending to refresh yourself. You look at your reflection in the water.

Instead of your own face you see the image of a lioness. Then the image changes and you see your own familiar face gazing back at you. However, you know that the power of the lioness is now a part of you and will always be there when you need to call on it. You dip your hands in the pool, splashing the water over your hands and face, feeling refreshed and energized.

Thoughts come to you of how this experience has benefited you, how it can help you through any difficulties you may be experiencing in your life. You know that now you have the ability and confidence to dispatch any enemy, if you choose to, in whatever form they appear.

When you are ready to depart, return to the garden by visualising the central tree clearly. This is your beacon and your guide. Be aware that a part of yourself remained there while you were travelling. It was and is your anchor. Return to that part of yourself simply by thinking this. You find yourself standing beneath the tree, feeling calm and refreshed. Return to normal consciousness and open your eyes.

Goddesses of Chaos and Ecstasy

Vintage fairy tale illustration

Wild Women

Chaos and ecstasy are intertwined, particularly in the most fundamental of human drives – the compulsion to procreate. Nature has made us that way. If we were incapable of desire, we'd have no impulse to reproduce. Nature's prime directive is for the continuation and evolution of species on this world. And how better to ensure procreation takes place than to make it ecstatically pleasurable? Perhaps we can't speak for animals, birds and fishes but for humans, desire is intensified by the emotion our brains create to go with it – love. Even the earliest civilisations were aware of love's destructive power. Nations toppled because of it. Lives were ruined. It is a chaotic force, sometimes horrific. There was no doubt in people's minds that beautiful and terrifying gods and goddesses must be behind it.

Chaos also refers to the primordial soup that was imagined to exist before matter was created. Life rose in ecstasy from chaos, again in the forms of gods and goddesses.

There are different kinds of Chaos and the four goddesses chosen for this section reflect its varying aspects. One of them is love, and who better to personify this than the Greek Aphrodite, who at the core of her being was dark indeed. Eris was a contrary goddess, who created strife and chaos, now reimagined as a more playful entity. Tiamat was a monstrous creature of the primal deeps, while Erzuli Danto, an African goddess, had and has many different aspects, some of them coquettish and mischievous, others deadly and terrifying.

Knowledge of the mysteries of these goddesses brings insight and strength – and awareness of the darkness of certain emotions.

Eris by Danielle Lainton

Eris
Strife, Striving and Mischief

*I am chaos. I am the spirit with which your children
and clowns laugh in happy anarchy.
I am alive, and I tell you that you are free.*

from '*Principia Discordia*'
by Omar Khayyam Ravenhurst

In Greek mythology, there are two version of Eris, the goddess of Strife. One is seen as more benign than the other. Strife has, in fact, two very different interpretations. The Greek writer Hesiod wrote as follows in his 'Works and Days':

'So, after all, there was not one kind of Strife alone, but all over the earth there are two. As for the one, a man would praise her when he came to understand her; but the other is blameworthy: and they are wholly different in nature. For one fosters evil war and battle, being cruel: her no man loves; but perforce, through the will of the deathless gods, men pay harsh Strife her honour due.

'But the other is the elder daughter of dark Night (Nyx), and the son of Cronus who sits above and dwells in the aether, set her in the roots of the earth: and she is far kinder to men. She stirs up even the shiftless to toil; for a man grows eager to work when he considers his neighbour, a rich man who hastens to plough and plant and put his house in good order; and neighbour vies with his neighbour as he hurries after wealth. This Strife is wholesome for men. And potter is angry with potter, and craftsman with craftsman and beggar is jealous of beggar, and minstrel of minstrel.'

Translation by Hugh G. Evelyn-White, 1914

The daughter of Nyx is the benign aspect. The other Eris is the trickster who brings chaos and disaster. Both of these goddesses are expressions of 'states', as were all the other children of Nyx. Most of the Greek gods had later Roman counterparts and Eris is no exception. She's Discordia in the Roman tradition.

Eris has a direct counterpart in Harmonia – whose name surely needs no explanation – and the Roman version of her was Concordia. Another Greek writer, Homer, associated Eris with a war goddess named Enyo – who also has a Roman counterpart in Bellona.

In Hesiod's work '*Theogony*', he lists the children of Nyx's daughter. They are another collection of 'states' and uncompromising in their aspects. We have, as Hesiod describes them: painful Ponos (Hardship), Lethe (Forgetfulness), Limos (Starvation), the tearful Algae (Pains), Hysminai (Battles), Makhai (Wars), Phonoi (Murders), and Androktasiai (Manslaughters), Neikea (Quarrels), Pseudea (Lies), Logoi (Stories), Amphillogiai (Disputes), Dysnomia (Anarchy), Ate (Ruin), and Horkos (Oath), who 'most afflicts men on earth, who are then willing to swear a false oath'.

The less fearsome Eris could be said to represent Striving rather than Strife – a desire to better yourself, keep up with your friends and family, acquiring all the consumer goods advertising might insist you need for a full and perfect life. In moderation, that impulse isn't a bad thing – it impels us to take action, and, as in Hesiod's example above, encourages us to get to our modern equivalent of plough and field. She can be seen as Order rather than Disorder. But the other Strife is a different matter. She is Discord and her presence splinters Harmony.

Eris the Cruel is she who appears in Homer's '*The Iliad*', as the sister of the war god, Ares, and therefore the daughter of Zeus and Hera. Eris is responsible for starting the Trojan war, because she was offended by a snub.

Three other goddesses of Olympus – Hera, Athene and Aphrodite – had been invited along with other gods and goddesses of Olympus to the arranged marriage of Thetis and Peleus, who would later become the parents of the great hero Achilles. Eris was not invited, because she had a reputation for being troublesome. She was so put out by this, she decided she would show them just how much trouble she could cause. She stole into the wedding party and tossed a golden apple in among the guests. The apple was inscribed with the words 'For the most beautiful'. Hera, Athene and Aphrodite began to argue about who was the fairest among them. Zeus, attempting to calm the situation (although one old story suggests the whole situation had been carefully organised by him for his own purposes), asked Paris, the prince of Troy, to judge the three goddesses and decide who was the fairest. Hera, Athene and Aphrodite took off their clothes in order to try and beguile the unfortunate prince. They also attempted to bribe him. Athene offered the greatest wisdom, while Hera offered immeasurable political power, but Aphrodite – well, she was the goddess of Love, and Love is the trickiest of all states – she offered the most beautiful woman in the world. This was Helen, the wife of Menelaus, King of Sparta. A more prudent prince might've chosen power or wisdom, but Paris's choice of Helen doomed his city of Troy, which was defeated in the war that followed Helen's abduction. Perhaps Eris, mistress of discord, had known the inevitable outcome. She can be seen here as similar to the cruel fairy in the old tale 'Sleeping Beauty' – offended by not being invited to a big event (in that case, the Princess's christening), and unleashing the wrath of her vengeance thereafter.

There are other stories of Eris's trouble-making in

Greek mythology. Strife causes breakdown, war and ruin. The tales illustrate this precisely.

The Eris of Strife, then, is the shattering principle that disrupts Harmony with devastating and far-reaching effects. The Eris of Striving is the impulse to acquire, to become better. We could say a person needs to overcome the vengeful aspect of Eris in order to achieve the positive state of self-evolution.

In modern times, and separate to pagan belief of the Western Tradition, Eris has become the patron goddess of a religion known as Discordia, which was created in the 1950s by Gregory Hill and Kerry Wendell Thornley, using the names Malaclypse the Younger and Omar Khayyam Ravenhurst. Discordia can be seen mainly as an irreverent parody of religion, and within it Eris is more of a trickster who can occasionally be somewhat spiteful and contrary rather than a dark force. The Discordian interpretation of Eris challenges the philosophical obsession of trying to impose order upon the chaos of reality, where order equates to truth. The Discordians believe that truth can only be found in chaos, perhaps *is* chaos, and that the concepts of order and disorder are temporary filters through which chaos is viewed. They refer to this as the Aneristic Illusion, Aneristic equating to Order, while Eristic equates to Chaos.

Reflecting the very earliest forms of the goddess, the Discordian Eris – and her twin sister Aneris – represent the fluctuating states of chaos and order, a theme which permeates at some level all the belief systems of the world.

We can view Eris as a being symbolising freedom. She can represent an instinct to avoid rigid conformity, dogma, pettifogging authority and other such nonsense, which some regard as 'order' and a desirable thing. But this vision of order only stunts growth and promotes stagnancy. If you adhere to a rigid ideology you cannot continue to grow. Thoughts become as inflexible as the rules that govern you. Questions can no longer be asked, and, in effect, the soul and the mind cease questing. Obviously, we do need order in our lives, otherwise it would be very difficult to live in society, but there is a difference between acceptable order and repressive belief.

As the author Robert Anton Wilson once said, 'Belief is the death of intelligence. As soon as one believes a doctrine of any sort, or assumes certitude, one stops thinking about that aspect of existence.'

Working with the idea of Eris can help you free yourself from the lies and illusions of restrictive conformity. In the following pathworking, you will meet Eris at her most unpredictable and mischievous.

Meeting Eris

Begin the pathworking by entering the Garden of Gateways. To meet with Eris, you will go into the eastern part of the garden, seeking the changeable and dynamic element of Air, symbolising the chaotic nature of this goddess.

Take the appropriate exit from the centre of the garden and follow the path to the eastern area. You pass through the gate into a new environment.

Your first impression is of rushing air; movement all around you. It is a weird landscape, somewhat difficult to perceive, because all its components are constantly shifting with peculiar perspectives. You see mountain ranges morphing into what appear to be fractal patterns.

Winds rush past you, that seem to be particles of information, or of sand or of burning motes. This is the pattern of the world, of life itself, and it is chaotic.

You begin to move through this environment, perhaps at one moment walking in open landscapes, while at other times flying through strange buildings, or else slithering as a serpent along the streets of a bizarre city, the appearance of which is constantly changing. Yet, as you progress, you begin to perceive order in the randomness of things. It's as if chaos and order are in a strange and intricate dance, and one cannot exist without the other. From a random pattern, order emerges, only to disperse into a billion motes of energy. You find yourself moving through a wild landscape and perceive the constant shift of the seasons, as if time has sped up so that a season passes in a couple of seconds.

From this constantly evolving and changing soup of possibilities, you become aware of how this applies to your own life. You don't remain the same. Opinions mutate, preferences take a new course. You change your mind about situations and people constantly. You realise that *information* changes things. It can be seen as one of the living forces of the universe. This is a priceless currency in life.

Eventually you come to a structure that is composed of iridescent motes. It's immense. A temple or a palace. You pass into it, amazed by what you see, the constant dance of life. There are sounds that might be music or the song of creation itself. Clangs, ringings, strange sibilances and resonant tones. Dissonance turns to harmony turns to cacophony. Order and disorder forever whirling in the crazy ballet of creation.

At the centre of this astounding edifice, in a chamber of light, shadow, electricity, fire and unravelling mists, hangs the form of a tall woman. She is incredible to behold. Her dark eyes remind you of the softness of feathers, as deep as the reaches of eternity. Galaxies seem to swirl within their depths, as if you look through a telescope to a far horizon. Her body is made up of a dizzying waltz of atoms and stars, while her wild and swirling hair is composed of the fire of pure energy. When she speaks, rainbows flash and roil around her. Some of the colours within them are not of our reality. Eris speaks in sound, but also in colour and aromas. You see her words unfurling from her lips like ribbons of musical script, or of algebraic formulae, or the ancient symbols of magic.

Eris speaks, and it's as if a dozen voices and musical instruments make the sound: 'I am Chaos. My mystery is the revelation that both order and disorder are concepts of the human mind and only exist there. The hidden truth is the inexpressible exuberance of life. I am Chaos, the substance from which artists and scientists draw rhythms and dreams. I am the spirit with which children laugh spontaneously and see wonder in all things. I am Chaos. I am alive, and I am here to tell you that you are free.'

Once you hear these words your entire being explodes into a cascade of light, sound and colour. You feel as if countless universes exist within you. If you rise above the limited concepts of reality, which humans have imposed upon their existence, you can see you really are free. Everything is petty in comparison to the immense and incomprehensible powers of the multiverse, that endless tumble of creation and destruction of chaos and order. It is splendid, even if you can't truly comprehend it. It is pure beauty and Eris is its expression, with which we can communicate.

The goddess weaves visions upon the scattering air – scenes from your own life observed from different perspectives. You can see so clearly now there is no absolute truth, only perspective. Eris tickles you into perceiving everything through the eyes of a child, not just *your* younger self, but the archetype of the most innocent yet wisest child, uncontaminated by the trials of human life. This child is undisappointed, unhurt, unchained. This is part of you and is no small defenceless thing to be sheltered and protected. It is immensely powerful – far more powerful than your day to day self. It perceives, however, that you – being sometimes a small defenceless thing – needs *its* shelter and protection. It creates order from disorder, a world for you to live in. As you realise this, you hear the goddess laughing across many realities and universes.

Spend some time exploring the realms of infinite possibilities. Walk with Eris. She might appear to you in many forms and take you to many places. Go where you will.

When you are ready to depart, return to the garden by visualising the central tree clearly. This is your beacon and your guide. Be aware that a part of yourself remained there while you were travelling. It was and is your anchor. Return to that part of yourself simply by thinking this. You find yourself standing beneath the tree, feeling calm and refreshed. Return to normal consciousness and open your eyes.

Essence of Eris by Storm Constantine

Aphrodite by Danielle Lainton

Aphrodite
Mistress of Wild Desire

Idalian Aphrodite, beautiful!
Fresh as the foam, new-bathed in Paphian wells,
With rosy slender fingers backward draw
From your warm brow and bosom your deep hair…

From an ancient Hymn to Aphrodite

Aphrodite is most commonly known as a goddess of love and beauty, a member of the Ancient Greek pantheon who resided upon Mount Olympus. In the many myths involving her, she's often presented as vengeful, jealous and petty, distributing curses and punishments against mortal men and women for perceived slights against her – not least them choosing other goddesses to revere rather than herself. But this notion of Aphrodite fails to encompass all of her aspects, the roots of which go further back than Classical Greece. It's thought that Aphrodite derives from the syncretism of a number of goddesses who were revered throughout the Mediterranean and the Middle East in ancient times, such as the Egyptian Isis, the Mesopotamian Ishtar, the Phoenician Astarte, the Canaanite/Egyptian Qetesh and the Sumerian Inanna, among many others.

In the Greek myths, there are two stories concerning Aphrodite's birth or creation. In one version, from the poet Hesiod's *'Theogony'*, the god Uranus was castrated by his son Cronos and the severed genitals were thrown into the sea. The water foamed and roiled about them, mixing with the semen of the mutilated god, and from this fluid Aphrodite was created. She rose fully-formed from the sea, a perfect, lovely creature. Her name is said to mean 'risen from the foam'. Hesiod tells us she came ashore at Paphos, on the island of Cythera, which became one of her greatest cult centres, where she was known as Aphrodite Cytherea. The other version of her creation, found in Homer's *The Iliad*, describes her as a daughter of the god Zeus and the Titaness Dione.

These aspects of Aphrodite are sometimes seen as separate goddesses, the daughter of Uranus being Aphrodite Ourania (or Urania), patroness of divine and transcendent love, and the daughter of Zeus being Aphrodite Pandemos, a deity presiding over the sexuality of mortals and particularly erotic love – the lust that drives the reproduction of species. But these can be viewed as different aspects of the same deity.

As well as being a goddess of desire, pleasure and procreation, Aphrodite had other, intriguing aspects that are alluded to in her many epithets, of which here is a selection: Melaneis – 'the Dark' (perhaps of night), Nicephorus – 'Bringer of Victory', Areia – 'of Ares, and therefore of War', Tumborukhos – 'Gravedigger', Androphonos – 'Killer of Men', Epitumbidia – 'She upon the Graves', Summakhia – 'Ally in War', Machanitis – 'Deviser, Contriver', and Apaturus – 'Deceptive One'.

In Cythera, she was a kind of triple goddess: Aphrodite Ourania, Aphrodite Pandemos and Aphrodite Apotrophia. The last form meant 'the Expeller' and in this aspect she was believed to dispel evil from people's hearts.

It's clear from some of these epithets that she had a warrior aspect or was associated with war. In one myth, she was married to Hephaestus, the god of blacksmithing, but had a number of lovers, among them the war god, Ares. She was also the lover of the beautiful youth Adonis, who was gored to death by a wild boar.

Aphrodite had many children through her various love affairs, too many to list here, but below are a selection of those whose attributes are closest to their mother's.

Through Ares, Aphrodite became pregnant with the twins Phobos and Deimos. Their names meant 'fear and panic' and 'terror and dread'. They were said to fight alongside their father in battle and are believed to represent the fear of loved ones involved in conflict dying in combat. Ares and Aphrodite also had a daughter, Harmonia, who represented marital harmony.

The god of wine and intoxication, Dionysus, fathered Iakkhos, who became a divine figure in the Eleusinian mysteries. Priapus, a god renowned for his large, constantly erect phallus, has uncertain parentage. He was fathered either by Adonis, Dionysus or Zeus – accounts vary and may be down to local variants on the myth.

Hermaphroditus, an extraordinarily beautiful young man, was the offspring of Aphrodite and Hermes. The naiad Salmacis fell desperately in love with him, but he rejected her advances. She prayed to the gods that they should be united as one for eternity. Her wish was granted, and the pair merged into one being who was half male, half female. The term hermaphrodite derives from the god's name.

Eros, the winged youth of love who fires the arrows of desire into human hearts, and his twin brother Himeros, the god of desire, were in some accounts said to be already growing within Aphrodite's body when she was created from the severed genitals of Uranus. The *Erotes*, the winged demi-gods of love were also her sons and often accompanied her. Among them was Pothos, the spirit of sexual longing.

All of the offspring mentioned here are in some way connected with love, lust or longing.

Aphrodite is regarded as the patron goddess of prostitution and it's believed that hetaerae, or sacred prostitutes, were connected with her cult. The idea of sex as a sacred act is a recurring theme in ancient belief systems and as Aphrodite was particularly associated with love-making it seems appropriate that sex in her name would have been regarded as blessed by her, or it might simply have been conducted as an offering to appease her or seek her favour.

As Aphrodite is strongly connected with the sea, she had various forms associated with it. She was worshipped in sea caves, which people transformed into grottoes that were decorated throughout with shells. As a sea goddess, Aphrodite was depicted as wearing a fishing net as a veil or shawl. It's said that visitors to these shrines brought with them a ritual comb called a *kteis* as well as cowry shells (which can be regarded as symbols of the female vulva), and scallops.

As a benevolent goddess of sailors and sea travellers, she had the epithets Pontia ('of the Open Sea'), Limenia ('of the Harbour'), Pelagia ('of the Sea') and Euploia ('of a Fair Voyage').

Aphrodite is perhaps most famous for her role in Homer's epic *Iliad*, where she is chosen by the Trojan prince Paris as the loveliest of goddesses. For this judgement, she rewarded him with the most beautiful woman on earth – Helen, wife of the King of Sparta. But even as a gift from a goddess, Helen didn't come without a very high price. In order to claim his prize, Paris had to seduce Helen away from home, which united the Greeks in outrage and initiated the Trojan War. The goddesses Hera and Athene, judged by Paris to be less beautiful than Aphrodite, were so disgusted by this insult they supported the Greeks in the conflict and helped lead them to victory. Troy perished because of Paris's ill-fated, irresponsible and perhaps foolish desire for Helen.

Aphrodite epitomises the madness of desire, when sexual attraction turns to frenzy. She is the very thing that facilitates the continuation of life upon our planet. Without reproduction, all species would die, and the lust that drives all beings to want sex, and through that to reproduce, is personified in this goddess – desire that is inexpressively powerful, primal and irresistible. The influence of the love goddess could drive people mad.

All of us have heard stories, or have had experiences ourselves, of desiring someone so passionately it feels like a kind of possession, if not insanity. It's a craving that suppresses appetite and the ability to sleep. People can make extremely bad life choices when held in the clawed grip of such desire. It can be experienced as extreme pain, a devastating longing that can only be relieved by the presence – the attention – of the beloved, whatever the cost. Aphrodite is the embodiment of that primordial voracious force. She is ecstasy and she is emotional chaos.

But if you approach the least destructive of her aspects, you can connect with the unfettered joy of simply being alive, when existence itself is wild and ecstatic. Meet Aphrodite by night, upon the shore at the sweltering height of summer, and experience the passion of eternity.

Meeting Aphrodite

Begin the pathworking by entering the Garden of Gateways. To meet with Aphrodite, you will go into the western part of the garden to seek the element of water.

Take the appropriate exit from the centre and follow the path to the west, which leads to the water garden. As before when visiting goddesses of this element, follow the path down the waterfall.

At the foot of the falls, you emerge into a bright spring day, near noon. You are standing upon a hilltop, looking down over rolling green fields towards a sparkling blue sea. Even from here, you can smell the brine and hear the crash of the white breakers. Upon the hillsides are copses of tall poplar trees and through their branches you glimpse the brightness of white marble, where sylvan temples are concealed.

Breathe deep. The air is full of the perfume of hyacinths. Spring flowers grow riotously from the bright green turf. Sheep graze around you, tended by handsome shepherds clad in goatskins. You feel full of excitement and energy as you begin to walk down the hill.

This is Arcadia, the Golden Land in a Golden Age. It is a land of innocence, but not of piety. It is a world of hedonistic pleasures and simple joyous celebration. In this place, there are no dark corners, no stern repression, no guilt, no fear, no shame.

Creatures of myth bound out of the trees. You see proud centaurs racing down the hillside, their tails streaming in the wind, their long hair blown back from their faces. Some carry lyres, which they play as they gallop along. Others sing loudly. You know that they are being drawn to the feast of the goddess Aphrodite, which will take place upon the sea shore. You too are going to this feast.

As you walk in the warm air, enjoying its scents, you peer at the trees around you. Beautiful dryads, the spirits of the trees, emerge from the trunks. Their hair is of leaves and twigs and their skin is green. They too are going to the feast in their gowns of russet bark and viridian leaves.

Further down the hill, you come to a rushing stream that pours over the rocks. Its song is the alluring cry of the naiads, spirits of the water. You jump over the stream and see their strange faces looking up at you. The naiads are swimming down towards the ocean.

You glance up and see white winged horses soaring in the aching blue sky. Petals rain down from their mighty pinions.

You hear laughter behind you and turn to see a group of satyrs and maenads running down the hill towards you. The satyrs are playing upon pipes and the maenads rattle tambourines and as they race along, they leave a trail of flowers in the air that tumble from their bodies. They sweep you up among them and you are running and dancing with them, down towards the sea, surrounded by floating flowers and their rich perfume, enlivened by a wild and natural ecstasy.

Eventually, you reach a wide paved road and upon it ride the heroes and heroines of myth. You see the Amazon queen Hippolyta, with her magical golden girdle. You see Theseus, the king of Athens who fought the Minotaur. There are many others you might recognise as well as figures who are unknown to you but are nevertheless intriguing. Among these are more bizarre individuals, who are monstrous in some way – a minotaur, demonic figures – yet all are caught up in the riotous, joyous atmosphere of Aphrodite's festival.

Now, amid a great boisterous crowd, you dance upon a path that leads down through the rocks towards the sea. A multitude of people and creatures have already gathered there, before a large cave, whose entrance is draped with green weed and adorned with shells. There is a sense of great anticipation, but now the gathering falls silent. The sun is sinking down the sky.

Amid a glimmer of torchlight, a tall slim figure comes forth from the shadows of the cave. You realise this is Aphrodite herself. She's surrounded by the maidens and priestesses who always attend her, as well as the *Erotes*, the beautiful, winged youths who represent the capricious spirit of love.

You find yourself at the front of the crowd. Aphrodite is a voluptuous fair-skinned woman, covered with a veil of fabric that resembles a fine fishing-net, which is threaded with shells. Beneath it, you see she is robed in shimmering fabric, which is stitched with gold thread. Her attendants draw the veil from her and her hair tumbles over her breast in golden waves. You gaze into her deep, violet eyes and see at once that she recognises you, has always known you. She holds out her hands to you and you take them in your hold. A feeling of great ecstasy, peace, abandon, chaos and joy cascades through you all at once. You feel as if you too have wings, like the *Erotes*.

For a while you commune with the goddess, witnessing all the times in your life her influence has affected you for both good and ill. Yet despite the negative qualities of her aspects, you see her for what she truly is: a joyous shout of triumph over death. She is life, ever replicating, ever burgeoning. She is what lies beyond death: the recurring cycle, the urge to reproduce for all time, sustaining all creatures upon the Earth. The desire she brings is the elixir of life, whether it comes through a glance, a scent, a gasp of breath or the strike of an arrow through the heart.

Let the emotions course through you in all their shades and intensities. For this one pure moment, experience the core of life, its centre.

Eventually, the goddess releases your hands and you become aware of your surroundings once more. Evening has fallen, and Aphrodite is now crowned with stars. Those who have gathered to attend her festival are feasting and drinking around you, and with a smile, she gently pushes you away, indicating you should take part in the revels.

The moon rises high and casts a road of light across the ocean. Many of the celebrants play musical instruments, and all are dancing, while voices rise in joyful, bawdy song.

Gradually, you notice members of the throng running off into the night, back to the hills and fields. You hear the distant cry of a hunting horn and are drawn to follow. All the creatures of this mythical world are at play in the light of the moon, and you join with them. Go now and do what you will. Enjoy this world of freedom and pleasure. It is your time.

When you are ready to depart, return to the garden by visualising the central tree clearly. This is your beacon and your guide. Be aware that a part of yourself remained there while you were travelling. It was and is your anchor. Return to that part of yourself simply by thinking this. You find yourself standing beneath the tree, feeling calm and refreshed. Return to normal consciousness and open your eyes.

Erzuli Danto by Danielle Lainton

Erzuli Danto
Mother of Freedom

Richard Ward

*'Oh Erzuli Danto, woman of my good luck,
I am calling you, priestess,
for you to bless the charm.
The priestess Erzuli controls the charm.
Oh Erzuli Danto, woman of my good luck,
I'm calling on you, the magic is spreading!'*

(English translation from the original Kreyol
of a sung petition to Erzuli Danto)

Erzuli Danto, the 'black Erzuli', is a vodou lwa, an ancestral spirit from Haiti in the Caribbean. Since the 17th century, when Africans from many different tribal nations were taken to Haiti in chains, Erzuli has been venerated there. Haitian vodou is a religion which pays homage to those many different natural and ancestral spirits. It is a complex amalgam of various rites and traditions with its own magical language; it has many branches, and that to which Erzuli Danto belongs – the Petwo rite – is the most complex of all.

Unlike other vodou rites, Petwo was purely Haitian born, incorporating spirits from Dahomean, Nigerian, Kongolese, European, and indigenous roots. Within the Petwo rite, all of these incorporated deities are characterised by an aggressive nature, which in many cases is one not shared with their African antecedents but is common amongst many spirits from the Kongo tribes whose influence on Petwo is the most considerable. Although the form of Erzuli known as Danto may not be of great antiquity, her African origins among the Fon of Dahomey are far more ancient. Here she was Azili, an ancestral serpent goddess.

In common with other Petwo lwa, Erzuli Danto is strongly associated with the element of fire. All forms of Erzuli are strong female personalities, but whereas her Dahomean form in Haiti is young, coquettish and playful, the Petwo transformation has rendered Erzuli Danto a fierce warrior mother. According to Haitian folklore, it was she who was called upon in the vodou ceremony performed at Bwa Kayman in 1791, a pivotal act in the guerrilla war for her devotees' independence from their European overlords. This is why she earned the epithet 'Mother of Freedom'. Considered to be the mother of all Petwo lwa, this often-overlooked deity is of immense importance within not just the magi-religious history of Haiti, but its political one, having been a key part of an indispensable force that, in 1804, established the first independent Black Republic in the Western hemisphere.

Like all lwa, her chief manifestation in the physical world is through possession of her devotees during ecstatic ritual. Following various opening acts of ceremony and the opening of the way between the worlds by the gate-keeper, a Petwo form of the spirit Legba, Erzuli Danto is called through the casting of her veve or 'sacred symbol', given offerings of pork and plantains to eat, rum to drink, and cigarettes to smoke if she wishes. Songs of her are sung, and dancing commences to the strange off-beat of the Petwo drums. The spirit then temporarily possesses her chosen devotee(s) and uses them as a conduit to converse with others.

Strange as it may sound, the most common depiction used to represent Erzuli in Haiti, are lithographs of the Madonna, these commonly include both classic images of the Virgin Mary, and the Mater Delorosa, whose daggers pierce her own heart in sorrow. As the African slaves were forced to convert to Catholicism and vodou was outlawed; the idea of syncretism of the lwa with Catholic saints was born. Within many of the images of the saints, the slaves recognised aspects relating to certain lwa present in their iconography. Erzuli Danto is most often represented by the Black Madonna. Proudly bearing her scars, she was the perfect image through which Erzuli Danto could be clandestinely venerated.

Erzuli Danto's personified appearance in folk tradition is that of a beautiful, strong mature African woman dressed in dark blue attire with a red scarf tied around her neck, symbolic of her fiery Petwo nature. She carries a dagger in each hand, ever ready for battle if the need arises, and like all forms of Erzuli, has a fondness for perfumes and jewellery. Women and children are particularly sacred to her, and she is traditionally sought for protection, particularly by sorcerers, as it is they who enlisted her help on that memorable night in 1791, and she continues to protect her devotees to this day.

Meeting Erzuli Danto
Richard Ward

As before, enter the garden of gateways and walk towards the southern part of the garden. Note that this time you are carrying a small straw bag. As you progress through the formal landscape and open the gate that lies deep within the southern part of the garden, you emerge to find yourself on a dirt road in a hot climate.

The air is humid, and the dying embers of daylight rapidly disappear as the sun sets below the horizon. You approach a crossroads, similar tracks stretch left and right, but the one straight ahead is narrower, not much more than a path that barely pierces the dense tropical foliage.

On the left of the road ahead, a lone tree extends skyward at the edge of the crossroad. As you draw closer, you see white candles burning around its base, offerings of food, cigars, coins and bottles of cane alcohol placed amongst its gnarled roots.

As you approach the crossroads itself, you notice a strange symbol drawn in white powder on the ground at the centre of the crossroads, its outline intermittently illuminated by the cluster of small flickering flames. This is the veve of Kalfu, a Petwo form of Legba, the guardian of the night roads who must first be appropriated in order to approach Erzuli Danto herself.

You pause by the tree, open your bag, and place some of the offerings from it among the roots, along with a few coins from your pocket. A tall, young, stern-looking Haitian man dressed entirely in black emerges from amongst the shadows at the edge of the path ahead. Once more you reach into your bag, taking out a bottle of rum and a large cigar and hand these to him with the greeting 'honour and respect for the night'.

Veve of Kalfu

His demeanour changes and he cracks a smile and hands you a small smooth stone, which you place in your bag or pocket. Kalfu allows you to pass through the crossroads as his fleeting liminal form melts back into the encroaching darkness.

As you walk straight ahead, the path begins to open out a little, and you become aware of the sound of drums in the distance, and then raised voices as you draw closer to their source. Soon, you notice the flames of torches dancing amongst the trees. The path further widens and you see the hint of a clearing ahead. Eventually you can perceive the shadows of people dancing to the strange disorientating but powerfully hypnotic beat of the Petwo drums. Intermittently lit by flaming torches that surround the clearing, you notice that there are men and women, all dressed in white with red head scarves and sashes.

Veve of Erzuli Danto

You move into the clearing and make your way through the throng of dancers to the old tall tree in its centre. Once again, candles placed around its twisted roots dimly illuminate offerings. You note another veve traced upon the ground. This is the symbol of Erzuli Danto. You reach into your bag once more and take out the offerings of food, cigarettes, rum and perfume that you have brought for her and place them alongside those already present.

You turn to gaze upon the dancers, and a stern but beautiful mature Haitian woman dressed in dark blue with a red neckerchief approaches you, her jerky movements matching the rapid beat of the drums. Her eyes are rolled back in her head in a state of trance, the twin daggers she carries flash brightly. She is a mambo, a vodou priestess possessed by Erzuli Danto, and although she addresses you in Kreyol, your mind understands her as if she were speaking in your native language. Take time to commune with her, to ask her the ways of this warrior mother, to learn from her.

Finally, after a period of conversation, she asks you for something. You reach into your pocket and produce the small stone you were given earlier at the crossroads. Still possessed by Erzuli Danto, the mambo picks up the bottle of rum that you have left for her and takes a mouthful, spraying the liquid over the stone as it sits in your hand. She clasps your hand between hers as she rubs the sticky liquid over the talisman's smooth surface. She smiles. 'It is blessed,' she says. 'Carry it with you always and it will protect you from harm and bring good luck.'

You thank her and turn to leave as you came without looking back.

When you pass by the crossroads on your return journey to the garden, you notice the next day is just beginning as the first light of dawn barely breaks over the horizon. By the time you reach the garden itself, you can feel the gentle warmth of the rising sun as you once more stand before the tree at its centre, your journey to meet Erzuli Danto now at an end.

Tiamat by Danielle Lainton

Tiamat
Primordial Chaos

Ummu Hubur, who forms everything,
Supplied irresistible weapons and gave birth to giant serpents.
They had sharp teeth, they were merciless...
With poison instead of blood, she filled their bodies.
She clothed the fearful monsters with dread,
She loaded them with an aura and made them godlike.
She said, 'Let those who look upon them feebly perish,
May they constantly leap forward and never retreat.'
She created the Hydra, the Dragon, the Hairy Hero
The Great Demon, the Savage Dog, and the Scorpion-man,
Fierce demons, the Fish-man, and the Bull-man,
Carriers of merciless weapons, fearless in the face of battle.
Her commands were tremendous, not to be resisted.
Altogether she made eleven of that kind.

From the first tablet of the *Enûma Elish*

Tiamat is a primordial goddess in the belief system of ancient Mesopotamia. She symbolises the sheer chaos of the first creation and was said to have arisen from the ocean. Merging in a sacred marriage with the god Abzû, who presided over fresh water, she gave birth to other gods. This version of the myth depicts a serene form of the goddess. However, there are variations on the story.

In the Babylonian version of the creation myth, known as the *Enûma Elish*, initially there was only salt water, the ocean, symbolised by Tiamat, and fresh water, symbolised by Apsu (another name for Abzû). When these waters came together and blended, new gods were created: Lahmu and Lahamu, Anshar and Kishar, and finally Anu, who went on to create Ea.

Tiamat and Apsu are disturbed by these younger gods, who are too noisy for their liking. Apsu and Tiamat can't even sleep because of the row they make. Apsu particularly is so incensed by this he vows to destroy his children to give him some peace. Tiamat wants to be more lenient with them, but he ignores her pleas. However, Ea, the wisest among the young gods, discovers his father's plans and takes action to prevent it. Drawing a magic circle around himself, he works a spell that sends his father into an eternal sleep – effectively death. He then takes his wife Damkina into the deepest waters of the now motionless Apsu and there makes a home. His wife gives birth to a son. This is Marduk, who is extremely powerful, greater than all the other gods. He creates violent waves in the Apsu, which even disturb Tiamat in her sleep. This tips her over the edge. She is still furious over what happened to Apsu, and now resolves to go to war with the younger gods and end the matter once and for all. She creates a monstrous army of sea serpents and dragons and sets her first-born son, Kingu, as their leader.

Ea discovers what Tiamat intends, but knows he can't stop her alone. Neither can his siblings help. So he calls upon his son Marduk to prevent Tiamat destroying them all. Marduk agrees to this, but on one condition; he must become the supreme god who rules the universe. Desperate, all the other gods agree to his demand. They furnish him with potent weapons: a net, bow and arrows and a club. Marduk also has command of seven winds, which he uses to create a fierce storm and a flood. Mounting his chariot, pulled by four horses, Marduk charges into battle against Tiamat and her forces, taking the storm and the tempestuous flood waters with him. When he reaches the angry goddess, he challenges her to single combat. Outraged at his audacity, Tiamat attacks him, but Marduk is ready and captures her in his net. When she opens her mouth to scream at him, he throws the stormy winds into her face. The winds enter her mouth and gust down into her belly, which distends as they fill her. Marduk takes an arrow and shoots Tiamat's swollen stomach, causing her to burst apart. As she dies, her army attempts to flee, but Marduk again casts his nets and catches them all like fish. He takes the two parts of Tiamat and with them creates the heavens and the earth.

The grateful gods happily make Marduk their supreme leader. From the blood of Tiamat's son Kingu, mixed with earth, Marduk fashions human beings, which he intends to be servants to the gods. His divine family make for him a wondrous city to be his home; the city of Babylon.

Tiamat was said to have created eleven monsters to do battle with her children, which were described in the *Enûma Elish*. These were colourful-sounding creatures: Bašmu (the Venomous Snake), Ušumgallu (the Great Dragon), Mušmaḫḫū (the Exalted Serpent), Mušḫuššu (the Furious Snake), Laḫmu (the Hairy One), Ugallu (the Great Weather-Beast), Uridimmu (the Mad Lion), Girtablullû (the Scorpion-Man), Umū dabrūtu (the Violent Storms), Kulullû (the Fish-Man) and Kusarikku (the Bull-Man).

While Tiamat has a terrifying, chaotic form as the raging primordial waters, she's not always depicted as monstrous. One of her epithets was 'the glistening one', and she was regarded as the epitome of feminine beauty. Another of her epithets was Ummu-Hubur, which means the creator of all things. It's believed that in Mesopotamia, the female deities predate the males by considerable time, and some writers suggest that Tiamat may have sprung from the cult of Nammu, a primordial goddess of Sumeria, a watery creative force, who was also associated with the Underworld.

Tiamat was often described as having a tail, or as being a sea serpent or a dragon. She could be visualised as a rather savage mermaid. She eventually became known by other names, among them Thalattē, which is most likely associated with the Greek word *'thalassa'*, which means 'sea'. Some writers have connected her with the Greek sea goddess Tethys.

Meeting Tiamat

Begin the pathworking by entering the Garden of Gateways. To meet with Tiamat, you will go into the western part of the garden, seeking the great primordial ocean.

Take the appropriate exit from the centre and follow the path to the west, which leads to the water garden. As before when visiting goddesses of this element, follow the path down the waterfall.

You emerge upon a beach and there the waves thrash strongly against the shore. You look up at the bright stars of the southern sky. You know that the stars particularly associated with Tiamat are those of Cetus, the great Whale, which rides upon the river Eridanus.

To prepare for the meeting ahead, fortify your aura by visualising a protective egg of light around you, which you will and intend to be impenetrable. If you wish, you can reinforce it with whatever means you would normally use to shield yourself during meditation or ritual. This strengthened aura will act as your guardian for the experience ahead.

Now, take a deep breath and face the ocean. You sense that an immense creature is approaching in the distance.

You know it has come from a deep, far place. You expect a huge Kraken, or some other kind of sea monster, to rise from the turbulent waves.

Presently, a short distance from shore, you see a great threshing in the water, accompanied by loud splashing sounds. Something huge throws itself upon the sand, and lies still for a moment, seemingly covered in a blanket of weeds and flotsam. This, slowly, it rises, and you don't see a monster, but a giant of a woman. She's dripping with water, her body hung with swathes of seaweed, through which small sea creatures crawl. Anemones cluster upon her bare shoulders like jewels. Her hair, tangled with shells and weed, hangs to her waist. She is no sweet beauty but exudes the aura of a being who has been in the sea for thousands of years. Her hair is white, as if bleached and matted by salt. Her skin is greenish-blue. Fish both large and small swim all around her, their supple backs just breaking the surface of the water. You see, far in the distance, the vast forms of whales, the plumes of air they exhale, mixed with water so that it looks like steam.

You're aware that it is Tiamat towering over you, surrounded by her creatures. You know that another name for her is Thalassa and that she's a personification of all that lurks beneath the sea, of all the mysteries of the deeps that humankind have never discovered or plundered.

You ask Tiamat to reveal to you her mysteries. She bows her head in assent and reaches out to you, smiling secretively. Although you feel a twinge of unease, you know you must walk out to her, where she stands at the edge of the shore among the wavelets, where the sea meets the land, the mundane meets the mysterious. You take Tiamat's hand and she pulls you into the water. For a time, you wade awkwardly alongside her, until the water becomes too deep. Then the goddess pulls you beneath it.

If you wish to learn Tiamat's mysteries, you have no choice but to stay with her – trust her. Despite knowing this, for a while you struggle, fearing you'll drown, but then Tiamat seems to realise that this puny creature with her is suffering and grants you the ability to breathe underwater. At once, you feel at ease, confident to continue.

Now, still holding onto Tiamat's long hand you swim deep. She leads you to watery realms unseen by any human. There are vast ancient ruins of temples and cities, and you encounter the unimaginable creatures of the ocean depths. Some are alluring and beautiful to behold, like lovely mermaids, but then they reveal hideous fangs, or the cold, dead eyes of a shark, or spindly hands webbed like savagely-clawed fins. Some are more terrible creatures still, shadowy in the depths, like vast octopi and squids, occasionally with the repulsive hint of something human about them. Creatures large and small swim and flicker around you. Some are curious, some playful, some distinctly hostile. But the presence of the goddess beside you, plus the aura of protection you created, shields you from these denizens of the deeps.

You're aware that you're encountering entities that many cultures have believed in, both in the distant past and in the present day. They're extremely strong and to connect with them using their symbols, their associations, their connections, will bring you into contact with their original energy forms.

As you go ever deeper, the sights become more bizarre and the only light is phosphorescence from the ruins or from the sea creatures themselves. You feel great pressure on your body, not just of the weight of the sea, but of the millennia that have passed unnoticed here in this deepest of earthly realms. This makes you feel disorientated, even slightly intoxicated. You're aware that humankind once came from the deep waters, and as you peer into the murky depths, you can glimpse the stages of evolution playing out before your eyes. These creatures are your ancestors; you came from them. Tiamat whispers in your mind: 'All the truths of all time lie beneath the sea.'

You descend into the very soup of creation, the primordial waters of chaos where life first came into being.

Take some time to continue exploring, communicating with any entities and creatures should you encounter them.

When you're ready to return to normal consciousness, visualise the scene around you from the perspective of the garden, as if you've never left it. Visualise the central tree clearly, which is your beacon and your guide. Be aware that a part of yourself remained there while you were travelling. It was and is your anchor. Return to that part of yourself simply by thinking this. You find yourself standing beneath the tree, feeling calm and refreshed. Return to normal consciousness and open your eyes.

Tricksters and Crones

Adapted from a vintage illustration

Bogey Women

The scary crone who devours children, or tricks people, or inflicts unreasonable punishments on those who displease her is a common motif in fairy tales. But she's also found in pagan beliefs, where she was sometimes raised to the position of goddess.

Like the dark mother, the crone personifies the capriciousness of nature, the destructive power of storms, and the cruelties of a hard winter. Crones seem to inhabit winter as their natural season. Very few are found in sunny fields, although of course there are exceptions, as in the case of Black Annis, who can strike at any time of the year. They are rarely referred to as mothers, although mother goddesses are often referred to as crones. There is a difference.

The true crone inhabits the murky realm of where nature interfaces with reality. She is a supernatural creature who exists on the boundary of our world. You may come across her on a dark forest path, or in a blizzard or a thunderstorm. She is always incredibly ugly, sometimes with deformities. She wears rags and carries a staff. In the case of the Cailleach, she strikes the earth with her staff to sunder mountains and create valleys.

Because the crone is very old, she has immense wisdom, which she will sometimes share if she is in the mood or the right gifts are brought to her. You should never shrink from her hideous appearance, because that won't please her at all. The crone has the ability to appear young and beautiful, but for most of the time she chooses not to. Perhaps very few humans are considered worthy of being shown her more genial side, in both appearance and temper.

Baba Yaga by Ivan Bilibin 1902

Baba Yaga
Witch of the Wood

Then suddenly the wood became full of a terrible noise; the trees began to groan, the branches to creak and the dry leaves to rustle, and the Baba Yaga came flying from the forest. She was riding in a great iron mortar and driving it with the pestle, and as she came she swept away her trail behind her with a kitchen broom. She rode up to the gate of her chicken-legged house and said, 'Little House, Little House, stand the way thy mother placed thee. Turn thy back to the forest and thy face to me!' And the house turned facing her and stood still.

From *Vasilissa the Beautiful*,
a traditional Russian folk-tale

Baba Yaga is an ambiguous figure from Slavic folklore. She is said to live in a strange house in the forest that stands upon a single chicken leg (sometimes two) and can move around. The fence around her garden is made of human bones and adorned with skulls – believed to belong to those she has devoured. While she's associated with creatures of the forest, and has a motherly side to her, she can be capricious – a help or a hindrance. Her mood can change, so she must be approached with extreme caution.

The meaning of her name is elusive. The Baba part clearly derives from a Slavic word meaning 'woman', especially an 'old woman'. It can additionally mean 'grandmother', similar to 'babushka', the Russian term for grandmother, 'ancestor', and even 'midwife'. All are allusions perhaps to a perceived 'ancestral mother' or genetrix of a tribe or clan. Another suggested interpretation of Baba is that it means a vicious or ugly woman. The Yaga part, however, is more enigmatic.

Scholars have attempted to work out the etymology and have come up with several ideas by examining various Slavic tongues. Among these suggestions are that Yaga means terror, anger, shuddering, an eerie chill, a witch, or an evil wood nymph. Other proposals include the shedding of skin, or the act of skinning another.

Baba Yaga is predominantly a powerful witch with iron teeth. She's known as 'Bony Legs', because despite the fact she eats continually she's skeletally thin. She's said to move through the forest in a giant mortar, propelling her way along the ground, or through the air, with a pestle. When she's out in the forest, people are warned of her approach by the furious winds that surround her. The trees bend groaning into the wind and shed their leaves that whirl through the air. Baba Yaga might also be accompanied by a throng of shrieking spirits, who spin around her. Sometimes she's described as riding a mop or a broom. Her appearance is always terrifying, and extremely ugly. In one story, she lies across the top of the stove in her house, stretched in all directions, while her nose is so long it rattles against the ceiling when she snores.

Her chicken-legged house is also a moving vessel. It spins around as it travels, uttering blood-curdling screams, and can only be silenced and halted by the utterance of a magical incantation. If a potential visitor succeeds in bewitching the house, it will withdraw its chicken legs into itself and land on the forest floor with a crash. First, it will present its back to the visitor, but then it will spin round, and its front door will fly open. The windows of the house are eyes that see all. Should the visitor be desperate or brave enough to enter the abode of Baba Yaga, she will ask them an important question: 'Are you here of your own free will or were you sent?' The answer is crucial, since if it doesn't please her, she'll kill whoever stands before her.

According to the old stories, Baba Yaga has a variety of assistants. In particular, she is served by three mysterious horsemen: the White Horseman, the Red Horseman and the Black Horseman. She describes these individuals to one visitor as 'My Bright Dawn, my Red Sun, and my Dark Midnight'. Her other peculiar servants include three pairs of disembodied hands, who she refers to as friends of her bosom, and which appear out of thin air to do as she bids them. In some stories, the Baba Yaga are three sisters, of equal treachery and craftiness.

Tales of Baba Yaga typically involve people approaching her for help and having to keep on their toes to match her trickiness. If they fail, they will be killed and eaten. If visitors best her, they might get what they asked for and she will help them. In her more benevolent form (or perhaps mood is a better word!), she is an earth-mother, in control of the elements, and very wise. Nature itself is capricious, and she embodies that force. She can be kind or cruel. If she is approached by the pure in heart, who seek wisdom and knowledge rather than riches or vengeance, she will turn her kinder side towards them.

Baba Yaga is the archetypal Crone, the Witch Mother, or Mother of Bones. She is as unpredictable as the winds, a guardian spirit of the Waters of Life and Death. Approach her at your peril unless your heart is true.

Meeting Baba Yaga

Begin the pathworking by entering the Garden of Gateways. To meet with Baba Yaga, you will go into the northern part of the garden, seeking the element of earth, the ancient forests of the north.

Take the appropriate exit from the centre of the garden and follow the path to the cave in the north. As soon as you cross the threshold of the first chamber, the air grows moist and you're aware of a faint scent of earth and vegetation. You pass quickly through the cave and along a straight passageway, to emerge into a new landscape.

You find yourself on a narrow track at the edge of a vast, ancient pine forest – trees that have never been cut down by humankind. Behind you lies farmland, and beyond it forested mountains, but the farmland ends quite some distance from the pine forest. There is a border of rough scrub between the signs of civilisation and the wilderness.

It is daytime, but when you look into the dark, dusty depths of the forest before you, it could be any time of night or day in there. You hear rustlings and crackings, as if the trees are turning to observe you. Occasionally, you hear the coarse call of a crow. The prospect of walking the path ahead isn't very inviting. But you are here to seek the Witch Mother, and you know your heart must be true and steadfast. You know that Baba Yaga can take you to confront your shadow self in the depths of the forest, and you seek the knowledge you will gain from this experience. But you also know this will be a daunting task.

You venture into the forest and soon, when you look behind, you can no longer see the light of day. All is lit by a very gloomy, dim glow that seems to come from fungus on the ground or which grows on the trunks of trees.

You see a rider approaching along the path and are obliged to step off it so they may pass. You see it is a knight dressed in black armour, riding a black horse. His dark face is gaunt within his helm, and he glances down at you when he passes. 'I am the darkness that dissolves you,' he says, and then is gone.

You know he's one of Baba Yaga's servitors, and that he and his brethren represent different stages of human learning. For the personality to grow, for knowledge to thrive, first you must cast off all that you were. To symbolise this, you throw away your staff, which acted both to hack away undergrowth that often covers the path, but as a weapon too, should you require one. You also cast off your heavy cloak, which again was both a protection and a comfort in the darkness.

The forest seems to close in over and around you, and there is still no sign of the path leading anywhere. Now a white knight approaches along the path, glowing radiantly. He is beautiful and rides a white horse. As he draws near you see he carries a chalice made of crystal.

As he passes, he says to you, 'I am that which purifies you.' He throws the contents of the chalice over you, which at first burns like acid. You struggle to remove your smoking outer garments, until you are standing only in your underwear. Now, you feel very cold, but weirdly also refreshed and invigorated, filled with the energy to continue. Before you, the path stretches on.

Now, a red knight rides towards you upon a chestnut horse. His armour is metal but of a strange crimson colour that shines with immense brightness. You are reminded of the sky at dawn and before dusk. His face is swarthy and strong-featured, but he is smiling. He says to you, 'I am the light of the sun in darkness, and the vital force of life itself.'

With these words, he reaches down and hauls you up before him on the saddle. He turns his horse and it canters deeper still into the forest.

You come at last to a clearing, and here you see the bizarre abode of Baba Yaga. It is a house that stands on gigantic chicken legs, but it is spinning around madly. There is a garden of sorts, surrounded by a fence made of human bones, with skulls fixed on the palings.

The Red Knight puts you down from his mount and rides away.

Call out that you seek the wisdom of Baba Yaga, adding whatever words you think will calm the house and allow you to enter it. Use whatever wiles you can.

Eventually, the house heeds you and ceases its spinning, landing with a great crash, then settling upon its folded bird legs as if in repose, with its back to you. All the windows are shuttered, like eyes that are closed tight.

You feel it's safe to draw nearer and as you do so, the eyes of the house snap open – dark holes of unshuttered windows revealing nothing of what lies within. The house spins one more time and presents its front to you. The door swings open with an eerie creak.

Gathering your courage, you cross the threshold and find yourself in a large kitchen. A figure sits hunched at the huge old table, its face hidden by a ragged black shawl.

You tell this figure your purpose in coming here, at which it turns to face you and you stare into the grim, hideous visage of Baba Yaga. All that has been said of her is true. Her teeth, revealed in a cruel, leering grin, are made of iron. Her nose is long and pendulous, her hair like hanks of dead vegetation, and she is skeletally thin.

'Are you here of your own free will, child, or were you sent?' she demands.

To which you may reply: 'Both, since I'm here of my own will, yet sent myself.' (If some other response comes to you, you should say that instead.)

However you respond, Baba Yaga finds your words amusing and cackles.

'Then I have a use for you,' she says.

She stands and beckons for you to follow her. Outside, you find that a huge iron mortar has appeared – Baba Yaga's magical vehicle. She hops inside it, and beckons for you to join her. It's uncomfortably cramped within the hollow of this giant mortar. Uttering peculiar sounds and half garbled words, the Witch Mother commands the vehicle to rise. She indicates a large broom standing near to you. 'Sweep the path,' she says, then takes in her hands an immense pestle, by which she will guide the way.

Now begins a nightmare ride through the forest, during which you must sweep the ground behind the flying mortar to cover all signs of its passing. It's a difficult job since the mortar moves so fast, but you know you must obey the will of Baba Yaga if you are to receive her wisdom.

Now spend time experiencing this outlandish journey in your own way. Baba Yaga might speak to you as you travel, ask you questions about yourself. You must answer her with complete honesty and carry out whatever tasks she gives you.

In the night forest, you will find and face your own shadow self. This is your personal journey and cannot be described or predicted by anyone else. Once you have conquered your shadow self and have absorbed it into your being, so wisdom is given to you and you will emerge from your experiences in Baba Yaga's realm far stronger than before.

When you are ready to depart, return to the garden by visualising the central tree clearly. This is your beacon and your guide. Be aware that a part of yourself remained there while you were travelling. It was and is your anchor. Return to that part of yourself simply by thinking this. You find yourself standing beneath the tree, feeling calm and refreshed. Return to normal consciousness and open your eyes.

Black Annis, adapted from a vintage illustration

Black Annis
Child Stealer of the Hills

'Tis said the soul of mortal man recoiled
To view Black Annis, eye so fierce and wild.
Vast talons foul with human flesh there grew,
And features livid blue glared in her visage
Whilst her obscene waist,
warm skins of human victims close embraced.

From a description of Black Annis
By John Heyrick Jnr, (a Leicestershire poet, 18thC)

Black Annis is a supernatural hag within English folklore. She was said to have lived in Leicestershire, specifically in a cave among the Dane Hills that had an old pollarded oak tree at its entrance. She was fearsome to look upon, with a strange blue face, abnormally long teeth and iron claws. Some accounts say she had only one eye. She was said to have used her claws to dig out her cave from the soft sandstone of the cliff. She's had several names over the centuries, among them Cat Anna and Black Agnes.

Black Annis was a bogey woman used to frighten children into good behaviour. They were told the blue-faced crone stalked the countryside at night seeking children to devour. She could not appear during the day, because sunlight would turn her to stone. It was said that Black Annis could stretch her arms into houses and grab children from their beds, and that for this reason the cottages of Leicestershire had only one small window. Before eating her prey, Annis would suck out their blood, then remove their skins and hang them on her oak tree to dry out. After this, she'd tan the skins, so that she could fashion them into long skirts. She also had a taste for sweet young lambs, so any deaths among the local farmers' flocks was attributed to her. She was thought to be able to shapeshift into a large black cat and, until the late 18th century, folk customs we'd now find utterly repellent were enacted to celebrate the end of winter. It involved a mock hunt, when the body of a dead cat soaked in aniseed oil was dragged through the streets, pursued by hounds. This custom evolved into in a more acceptable form of celebration, which became the annual Dane's Hill Fair, on Midsummer's Eve. As part of the festivities, the Black Annis Women's Morris Dancers meet and dance in the spot where once Black Annis's Bower was said to lie.

While it was once thought that Black Annis derived from old goddesses, among them the Cailleach with whom she shares some attributes, modern writers are more inclined to think she was based on a real person, who earned rather a bad reputation, perhaps for no more than simply living as a recluse. A title deed remains from the 18th century which names a parcel of land as 'Black Anny's Bower Close'. Annis's cave was known as 'Black Annis's Bower'. The cave actually existed right up until the 19th century, but by that time it was neglected and starting to fill in naturally with earth. After the First World War, this historical site fell victim to town planning, and eventually a housing estate was built over it.

The writer Ronald Hutton, in his book *Triumph of the Moon*, goes so far as to suggest that Black Annis was based upon a woman named Agnes Scott, who lived in the Middle Ages. Agnes was a hermit (or anchoress), a Dominican nun who cared for the sick, specifically the inmates of a local leper colony. Agnes was born in a village called Little Antrum and was said to have lived a mostly lonely life of prayer among the Dane Hills. After her death, she was buried in the graveyard of a church in Swithland, in the Charnwood borough of Leicestershire, marked by a monument that was a veiled statue of her, wearing the black habit of her order.

It's possible that the truth of who Agnes Scott really was became distorted into the idea of Black Annis, because women living alone, and who were perhaps eccentric in appearance and habits, often became ostracised by the community and regarded as witches or monsters. Or maybe there really was more to Agnes Scott than met the eye!

Another possible origin for Black Annis derives from a 15th century wise woman, who allegedly foretold the death of Richard III. This woman, or sooth-sayer, was asked if she thought Richard had any chance of victory, and she replied that if his spurs struck the stones of the Bow Bridge that spanned the River Soar in Leicester, then bad luck would follow, and his head would strike the same spot. It's said that Richard did indeed ride over the Bow Bridge, as he travelled to the site of the Battle of Bosworth. And while he was crossing his spur did hit a stone of the bridge. Richard was killed during combat, and it was said that when his body was carried back across the bridge, his head did in fact strike the same stone. The bridge, which still stands in Leicester, was rebuilt in the 19th century. A plaque telling the story of Richard and the wise-woman is fixed to it.

Whatever her origin, Black Annis is now firmly a creature of myth and magic.

Meeting Black Annis

Caroline Wise

Begin the pathworking by entering the Garden of Gateways. To meet with Black Annis, you will go into the southern part of the garden, into midsummer.

When you emerge from the gateway to the garden, you find yourself walking along a road, an old straight track, ancient before the Romans. It is set between rolling hills in the South Midlands of England. The sun is setting at midsummer, and the darker part of the year will now begin, as the days shorten and the light decreases.

You see ahead a spectacle in the road. A side of sinister, women Morris dancers are performing in the road, their black and white and red costumes whipped up by a sudden wind. There is no music, just the sound of their bells and the noise as their sticks clash. There is a feeling they are summoning something, and you wonder what and why they are here.

You approach cautiously, wondering what the protocol is, as there is no space to walk past them at the side. Suddenly they halt the dance, and look at you, with sombre expressions, and part to the sides of the road, clearing the way. You walk through the two lines of silent dancers, and notice beyond them, up the hillside to your left, is a cave entrance, with a pollarded oak at the entrance. Looking back, you see the dancers are walking away.

From the cave slinks a supernaturally large black cat, a giant cat. As it descends the hill, it transforms into the form of an extremely tall, blue-faced hag, in tattered black clothes. She walks with a strange gait. Her long black hair is matted, and she wears a wide-brimmed hat. She is now on the road and coming towards you. A distant memory sparks you into terror – tales of Black Annis that you heard long ago, Black Annis who haunts this road. You can't scream: your voice seems stuck in your throat. You can't run, as your feet feel frozen to the ground. You see her gnarled hands now, and the long black talons of her fingernails. From her waistband hang skins and bones of people, of animals. You have no choice but to stand your ground.

Black Annis scoops you up and strides back to her cave. It seems like an enchanted cavern, glowing as the last rays of the sun catch on spider-webs or flashes of quartz in the rock. Skeletons of animals and birds lie on the floor. Black Annis speaks to you in a rasping voice.

'Today is midsummer, and the sunset shone into my cave, my yearly awakening. I rise as the devourer, as the darkness grows each day. I am nature red in tooth and claw, black in aspect, white as bleached bones. Now comes the time away from your tidy and pretty fantasy wheel of the year. Now comes the time of death.

'I am an echo of the times when there was no food for your animals, the beasts of the field; you will die. No food for the wild beasts, who may then devour you. You will die. I am the echo of death to your tribe. I am the echo of your fears of the dark – the monsters that ride the night, the stalker who knocks in the dark, the hungry wolf who circles your dwelling. I am the memory of the hard earth and the storm in the hills. I prowl as the black cat, a projection of your fears. But now made, I can't be put back in the box. I am here on the land in the time of the dark. And I stalk…Look.'

She holds out a polished black slate plate.

And you see kaleidoscope images appear, from the time of Palaeolithic hunters, who were unable to hunt in the storms, to the Neolithic farmers battling to keep their kin, and animals and settlements from destruction. Onwards in time, the images show people's constant struggle against the elements, of worshipping gods and beseeching. You see abandoned settlements and bodies that look no more than piles of rags. Trees are fallen, those which stand are bare. The fields are of stone. Forward in time the images come, resembling Bruegel's painting, 'Hunters in the Snow', which you finally understand. The coming of winter was not celebrated, it was feared, and the return of the hunt so keenly anticipated. The spectre of the hunters returning with sparse pickings was dreaded.

Black Annis continues: 'For you, I counsel, take the left-hand path, the road less travelled; walk the meandering path, the Old Straight Track, follow a star, or even forge a new way. But always take the Interesting Way. And do not stray from your true path. And one day you may be an echo for those who come after.

'For me, I will haunt this road, slinking as a cat, watching for prey, to suck the bones dry. To scare the children to bed, where they should be, safe and warm and protected from the elements. I will reveal my hag self as an echo to those with the Old Sight, like you. To those who scorn me, I will take my fill. I am the devourer.'

And she starts to sing a mournful song that lifts and dips in her rasping voice. You close your eyes and listen.

> *Sunset see my haglike guise,*
> *Night time when your fears arise.*
> *I am stalker of your fears,*
> *The terror when the cat appears.*
>
> *I am the Devourer.*
>
> *Face me down and stand your ground,*
> *I can show you why I'm bound*

*To linger at midsummer dusk,
On this road of old bone dust.*

I am the Devourer.

When you open your eyes, you are alone in the cave. Twilight is giving way to darkness, and a moon is rising outside. In this dim light, you see that the black slate plate is smashed on the floor. There are cobwebs everywhere, and the edges of the rock chamber are strewn with litter, blown in from the road. The skeletons that looked so dramatic before, are of a ra,t and a mouse, and a pigeon. Now, it doesn't look much like a witch's darkly enchanted lair, only rather bleak and depressing.

With a new-found respect for the spirit of the place, and an understanding of the dark period and its cumulative echo of the fear through time, you give thanks to Black Annis, and leave her a simple song, of your own making, from the heart, that you sing into her cave. Then you walk back down the hill, back along the road to the garden. And as you do, you hear the yowl of a cat. Or was it the wind?

When you are ready to depart, return to the garden by visualising the central tree clearly. This is your beacon and your guide. Be aware that a part of yourself remained there while you were travelling. It was and is your anchor. Return to that part of yourself simply by thinking this. You find yourself standing beneath the tree, feeling calm and refreshed. Return to normal consciousness and open your eyes.

The Cailleach by Storm Constantine

The Cailleach
Witch of Harsh Winter

*Her face was blue-black of the lustre of coal
And her bone-tufted tooth was like red rust.
In her head was one pool-like eye,
Swifter than a star in a winter sky.*

From *Scottish Lore and Folk Life*
by Donald MacKenzie, 1935

The Cailleach (pronounced roughly – and gutturally – Coy-ack) is a crone goddess from Gaelic mythology, found in many forms in the folklore of Scotland, Ireland and the Isle of Man. Primarily, she's a goddess of winter, and ushers in the winter months, thereafter presiding over them. One of her epithets is 'Daughter of the Little Sun', meaning winter. Her sacred plants are the holly and the gorse. She shares sovereignty of the year with the goddess Brìghde, who presides over the other half of the year. The Cailleach rules from Samhain to Beltaine.

In modern Gaelic, Cailleach means hag or old woman, yet in the ancient language her name meant 'veiled one'. The word can also refer to an owl, a sooth-sayer or a witch. Sometimes her name lengthens to Cailleach Bhéarach, which is said to refer either to her association with cattle, or else a word meaning shrill and sharp – perhaps a reference to the harsh winter winds. There are a variety of variations on this title, as well as completely separate names and epithets, found in different areas of the Gaelic-speaking lands. The word Carlin is associated with the goddess's name, meaning a witch or a wise woman, sometimes a harbinger of doom, like the Irish banshee (or Bean Sidhe).

In appearance, the Cailleach is described as a hag with

only one eye and rotten teeth. Her long, matted hair hangs over her face, or she is hidden by a veil. Yet, as with other crone goddesses, she has the ability to turn into a beautiful maiden, generally when someone is kind to her in her hag form: the kindness transforms her. She wears a plaid, or an enveloping cloak or shawl, and carries a magical wand or staff, known as a *slachdan*.

In Scotland, the Cailleach is regarded as the mother of all other gods and goddesses, who's credited with creating the mountains, hills and valleys. She was said to have dropped the mountains accidentally from the wicker basket she carries and is also believed to have shaped the landscape with her *slachdan*, carving out the valleys with powerful blows. She also uses this tool to control the weather.

 She's associated with the herding of deer, and patrols the landscape accompanied by herds of deer and wild pigs. There are several tales of her troubles with hunters. She may shapeshift into bird form, particularly sea birds, an eagle or a heron. If she strikes the ground with her *slachdan*, it freezes. And when the time of her rule comes to an end, she fights the arrival of spring. Every year, of course, she fails, and on Beltaine eve she turns into stone, and will remain that way until the months of her rule come around again in the early winter.

 There is a special day in the Gaelic calendar called Là Fhèill Brìghde. This is February 1st, the fire festival of Imbolc, dedicated to Brìghde, and the time traditionally when the transfer of power between the goddesses begins, as the first signs of spring start to appear. On this day, it's said the Cailleach goes out to gather firewood for the rest of the winter. If the day is fine, she can gather a lot of wood, which means that winter will last for longer. If the weather is bad, she won't gather much at all, or perhaps remains sleeping in her house, and people are relieved to know that spring will come on time.

In Scotland, a group of elemental spirits known as the Storm Hags or Cailleachan embody the destructive capabilities of nature. They are responsible for raising the wild storms of early spring.

One Scottish legend tells of how when the Cailleach washes her plaid (cloak) she brings in the winter. It takes her three days to wash this garment, and during that time the roar of an approaching storm can be heard from many miles away. When she has finished, her plaid is glistening white and the land becomes covered with snow.

There's another interesting myth about the Cailleach concerning the grain harvest. The first farmer to bring in his crops fashions a corn dolly from the last sheaf to represent the Cailleach. He tosses this into a neighbour's field, someone who's not yet finished gathering their crops. When this neighbour has completed the work, they'll then toss the dolly into another farmer's field. This goes on until it reaches the field of the last farmer to finish the harvest. They then have to keep the dolly for the entire winter, feeding her and giving her accommodation, meaning they have the Hag of Winter as a guest in their house until spring. No one wants this responsibility, as the Cailleach is a witch and unpredictable.

The Cailleach's influence is prevalent in mountainous areas, and many rugged, craggy sites are associated with her, as well as megaliths, rivers, lakes, marshes and wells. She is a mistress of storms and the sea, and a patroness of animals both wild and domesticated. Mountain springs were said to provide sanctuary for her as she travelled across the cold land, as in these places she could renew her strength and perform rites to control the weather.

As with many hag goddesses, the Cailleach can be benevolent or cruel. She is as wild and unpredictable as the harsh weather of winter or the destructive raging seas of the northern lands.

Meeting the Cailleach

Begin the pathworking by entering the Garden of Gateways. To meet with the Cailleach, you will go into the northern part of the garden, to the deepest, coldest part of winter.

Take the appropriate exit from the centre of the garden and follow the path to the cave in the north. As soon as you cross the threshold of the first chamber, the air grows bitterly cold and your breath plumes from your mouth in clouds. You pass quickly through the cave and along a straight passageway, to emerge into a new landscape.

You find yourself on a cliff path high above a dark and raging ocean. It is night-time and extremely cold. An icy wind is blowing fiercely, and you know that soon snow will come. It's dangerous to be out in the furious elements that are so wild and unpredictable. You could be blown to your death upon the black rocks below. You draw your heavy coat or cloak around you to protect you.

You're here alone in the darkness to learn the mysteries of the Cailleach. You know she can reveal secrets and grant boons to those who please her but can equally be cruel and vicious. There's no way of knowing, no precautions you can take, because this Hag of Winter is like the weather and cannot be controlled. The only thing you have to appease her is a gift – a basket of freshly-baked bread with butter and cheese. You feel you can't offer her meat because she might accuse you of slaughtering her deer and pigs, or the birds that are her companions.

As you trudge along the road, you utter a chant of your own devising to summon the Crone. The wind shrieks around you and now you can perceive shrill voices within it. There are also strange gruntings and snufflings.

Something charges across the path in front of you, a great many somethings. You see that it's a herd of wild pigs, making a screeching racket. They are followed by a shadowy herd of deer. It's as if these beasts have come up out of the sea. Once the animals have disappeared into the forested hills to the landward side of the road, you perceive a hunched dark figure standing some yards ahead of you. It leans upon a long staff, gripping it with both hands that appear almost skeletal.

You know this is the Cailleach. She has heard your call.

Showing no fear, no matter how you might feel inside, you bow to her and address her as 'Lady'. You tell her you have a gift for her, which you hold out.

The Cailleach beckons for you to come closer. Now you can see the hideous face, the one piercing eye glaring through the long, matted hair hanging over her face. She's dressed in layers of what seem to be rags, covered by an enveloping shawl of plaid. You gaze at her unfalteringly, as if she were the most beautiful creature on earth. You offer her the basket of food, from which she lifts the cover and inspects the contents.

Apparently satisfied, she nods and takes the basket from you. This she secretes somewhere in her voluminous clothing.

'Would you ride the wind, child?' she asks.

'That is my desire, great Lady,' you reply (you may instead use words of your own devising.)

Once she hears your reply, the Cailleach's tattered clothing billows up around her like wings, and she transforms into an enormous bird, a great black eagle. She throws back her head and utters a mighty scream. You realise she wants you to climb upon her back. Gathering your courage, you do so.

Now comes the wildest ride of your life. The Cailleach plunges into the wind, then soars up and up towards the mountains. The landscape rushes by beneath you, and you can see it now in its earliest form, before humankind developed. History tumbles past your inner eye, as the mountains rise and fall, glaciers shiver past, then the ice melts and forests crawl swiftly up the hillsides. The sea pounds and thrashes, eating at the coastline, which wriggles and shudders like a snake, its contours changing.

The Cailleach presides over the shaping of the earth, and also the weather that helps shape it. She is the winds, the rain, the snow, and her realm is the dark of winter, when the sun is weak. She doesn't represent sunlight or balmy days. Hers are the fiercest, darkest nights when uncanny creatures stalk the shadows, and the unwary traveller may vanish, never to be seen again.

The Hag of Winter is raw nature at its least forgiving, but the scream of the wind is triumphant, full of vigour and life. You can take this wild elemental force into yourself, remember it when you need to and use it to find strength and endurance. You can use your own will to shape concrete reality. This is the mystery of the Cailleach.

Spend some time with the Hag and go where she takes you. She might have many secrets to show you, within the hidden places of the mountains.

When you are ready to depart, return to the garden by visualising the central tree clearly. This is your beacon and your guide. Be aware that a part of yourself remained there while you were travelling. It was and is your anchor. Return to that part of yourself simply by thinking this. You find yourself standing beneath the tree, feeling calm and refreshed. Return to normal consciousness and open your eyes.

The Cailleach's Realm by Storm Constantine

Hecate by Danielle Lainton

Hecate
Mistress of the Crossroads

And she [Asteria] conceived and bore Hecate whom Zeus the son of Cronos honoured above all. He gave her splendid gifts, to have a share of the earth and the unfruitful sea. She received honour also in starry heaven and is honoured exceedingly by the deathless gods.

From '*Theogeny*' by Hesiod

Hecate, sometimes spelled as Hekate, is a goddess of the Ancient Greek pantheon, particularly associated with witchcraft. She was the only daughter of Perses and Asteria. Zeus was said to honour her above all other goddesses.

In ancient Athens, Hecate was a goddess protective of homes, who could bestow prosperity upon households and families, and drive away harmful spirits. But her main role is as a deity associated with sorcery and crossroads, with a knowledge of herbs and poison. She is also an Underworld deity. The precise meaning of her name is obscure, but some scholars have suggested it means 'she who operates from afar' or 'she who removes'. She shares attributes with the Roman goddess Trivia. One of her main cult centres was the city-state Lagina, where she was served in her temple by eunuchs.

In Greek art, Hecate is generally depicted holding two torches, or else other symbolic items such as keys, snakes and daggers. She can be shown as a young woman, dressed in a similar fashion to Artemis, with a short linen skirt and long leather boots – the costume of a huntress. In one account, she's described as 'wearing oak', while in another she wears a crown of oak entwined with serpents. She was commonly shown accompanied by dogs. In Egyptian papyri of the Ptolemaic period, Hecate's presence is described as being heralded by the barking of dogs, and she was referred to as a 'she-dog'. These creatures were also sacrificed to her, and their meat either eaten as a sacred food, or else left as offerings at crossroads. Other animals traditionally associated with her are the horse, the boar, the serpent, the cow and the wolf. A more modern association is the black cat.

Another common depiction of Hecate, especially in statues, was of a triple-headed goddess, and in this form she was the Goddess of the Crossroads. In one ancient document, she's described as having animal heads – that of a horse, a dog and a serpent. Very occasionally, she was described as having four faces, only three of which can be seen. Some writers suggest that the three visible faces represent the phases of the moon – the new, the half and the full. The invisible fourth face, which is always turned away from the beholder, thus represents the darkness that befalls the earth between the old and new moon. Another interpretation is that the three main faces represent three distinct goddesses – Selene, the moon in the sky, Artemis, the huntress on the earth and Persephone, the destroyer in the Underworld. In modern pagan belief, the triple goddess can also symbolise the female archetypes of maiden, mother and crone. Nowadays, the latter interpretation is the most common, although Hecate is recognised as a goddess in her own right. She's often regarded as the 'dark of the moon', the Mistress of the Night – essentially the fourth face of the moon that is hidden. Dark can be regarded as the moon's true state, since it's only visible when reflecting the light of the sun. Hecate is also dark in this way, so the ideas have become linked.

One of Hecate's attributes was as a goddess of the 'in

between', meaning doorways, city walls and their gates, borders of kingdoms, boundaries and crossroads, where a person crosses the threshold from one place into another. This also includes the crossing from life to death, from earth to the Underworld. Hecate was said to be a mediator between the realms, and this is reflected in some of her many epithets: Hecate Apotropaia (she who turns away or protects); Hecate Enodia (she who stands on the way); Hecate Propylaia (she who stands before the gate); Hecate Trioditis (she who frequents crossroads) and Hecate Klêidouchos (she who holds the keys).

Dogs too, one of the creatures sacred to Hecate, are important to the 'in between'. They guard thresholds, doorways and entrances, and the three-headed dog Cerberus guards the gate to the Underworld, ensuring the dead cannot leave nor the living enter it uninvited, before their time.

Shrines to Hecate were often placed at three-way crossroads. The Roman version of her, Trivia, means 'three ways', and in fact can be used as an epithet of Hecate, when she becomes Hecate Trivia, 'She of the Three Ways'. Even to this day, practitioners of magic and paganism see crossroads as places of power. Charms will be left at them or rites performed there, in the belief that the 'in between' will empower the magic.

As a goddess familiar with places or states of transition, Hecate was regarded as a protector for those who made crossings, either in the earthly realm or the Underworld. Her function was to deter destructive spirits from places or people over which she stood guard. This evolved into her being able to command such spirits and to use them for malevolent purposes.

Hecate is also closely associated with plants and plant lore, including the arts of herbalism and poison-making. She is credited with being a teacher in this respect, with the infamous witch Medea being one of her students. Her sacred plants and trees include mugwort, garlic, mandrake, aconite (which is also known as *hecateis*), belladonna, dittany, poppy, yew and cypress. The cypress tree is traditionally associated with the Underworld, and the yew is common in graveyards.

The description of a rite to Hecate can be found in *The Argonautica*, a fictional epic from Alexandria, dating back to 300BC. In this story, the Greek hero Jason wishes to appease Hecate, and learns of an appropriate rite from the witch Medea, who is a student and priestess of the goddess and knows how to approach her. She tells Jason he must bathe at midnight in a flowing stream, and then dress himself in dark-coloured robes. After this, he must dig a round pit, and sacrifice a ewe over it, by cutting its throat. The body of the ewe must be burned on a pyre standing next to the pit. Medea insists he must sweeten his offering with a libation of honey, and once this is done, he must leave the site at once, and not look back, no matter what he hears – even if that's the sound of approaching footsteps or the barking of dogs. We have to assume Jason followed these instructions and won the approval of the goddess.

Hecate is the mistress of the Keres, spirits of death, who were the daughters of Nyx. Along with Demeter and her daughter Persephone, Hecate was a prominent goddess of the Eleusinian Mystery religion, because of her connection with Persephone. As the mediator between the realms, and a protector of travellers who crossed the boundaries, Hecate was said to accompany Persephone every year on her journey to the Underworld.

Hecate is not associated with any male god, and there are no myths of her ever marrying or taking a lover. However, in some traditions, she's said to be the mother of a ferocious sea-monster named Scylla, who appears in Homer's '*The Odyssey*'.

Meeting Hecate

Begin the pathworking by entering the Garden of Gateways. To meet with Hecate, you will go into the eastern part of the garden.

Take the appropriate exit from the centre of the garden and follow the path to the eastern gateway.
    You emerge at night-time into a Mediterranean landscape, where the weather is warm. You are standing upon a road that passes through woodland, but this is not a dense forest. You have a sense of farms about you, and cultivated land beyond the trees. You feel there is a town nearby.

You are here to meet with Hecate, the Weaver of Fate – your fate in the future that will affect the past as well.
    Ahead of you there is a crossroads, and you become aware that the path you are walking now represents the past. The crossroads ahead is the 'now', the present moment, while the three other paths leading from it represents different futures, different opportunities.
    You reach the crossroads and see that offerings have been left there for the goddess, gifts of meat and red wine, as well as sprigs of her sacred plants and trees. You are attracted to the road that leads straight on into the east, to the new dawn, your destiny, but it's as if a barrier is placed before it, invisible but uncrossable. Before you make that journey you must first appeal to Hecate and ask her to reveal the path of destiny.
    You have your own offering to make and lay this alongside the others at the centre of the crossroads. You offer red wine and cake dyed red, which represent blood and fresh meat.
    Then a darkness crosses your vision. You blink, and

when you can see clearly again, a figure stands tall in front of you.

Hecate is a strange figure, comprising four women standing back to back. Her four heads represent the four phases of moon and one of these faces is always hidden. She is dressed in traditional Ancient Greek costume with a veil over her heads and long robes adorning her bodies. She appears very dark. It's not that her skin or clothes are dark, but that she *is* darkness; it surrounds her like a mist.

She has eight arms. In one hand she holds a flaming torch, in another a scythe or sickle, in another a snake, while in another she holds up a puppy made as an offering to her. You cannot see what else she holds for she remains motionless and you're unable to see her hidden side. Her expression is stern, yet not hostile.

Now you ask for permission to continue along your path and that she will reveal aspects of the future to you. You know that once she grants this permission, you will then walk beneath her influence.

Hecate tells you she will walk with you to the dawn. She has not only granted you permission to take the path but the privilege of her company. You find the crossroads is now behind you and a woman dressed in dark robes and veil walks at your side. She's now of normal height and appears to be a mortal woman, yet she exudes a powerful presence. A puppy trots at her feet, and in one hand she holds up a torch; a snake coils about her forearm. In her other hand she carries a sickle. She tells you the torch is to light your way and also to 'burn the fields', which means burning negativity from you. The sickle is to cut away 'dead wood', aspects, behaviours and notions you no longer need and that restrict or obstruct your personal growth. The snake represents her magical power, which you can call upon to affect reality, to make changes.

As you ponder on this, suddenly panic strikes your heart. At first you are puzzled as to why, then you see that at your side Hecate is transforming. Her shape is shifting in billows of smoke. She becomes a frenzied mare, its large teeth gnashing threateningly before your face, it eyes rolling in madness. Nightmares from childhood crash into your mind, and you flap your arms around your head in an attempt to banish them.

As these unsettling visions fade, relief is brief, for now Hecate changes form again. She appears in the form of a vicious three-headed dog. Here is Cerberus before you, the three-headed hound who guards the gates of the Underworld. Its foul hot breath assaults you, and putrid saliva drips from its fangs as it growls menacingly in your face. Memories of frightening stories read to you in early childhood rush in, whose terrifying characters you prayed would not find you in your bed. You remember how sometimes you were ashamed of the night terrors; they have forever haunted you.

The image of Cerberus fades away, and Hecate once more transforms, this time into an archetypal witch, proffering a cup to you. You fear it might contain poison, that if you should drink it you will die, or see more frightful visions, or you will change beyond return. Hecate gazes directly into your eyes. You reason that as you have willingly sought her company by entering her realm, you must trust her. Banishing caution, you take the cup and drink. It is a strange tasting brew, made from plants sacred to her. Immediately, you are calmed into a state of dreamy ambience, where deep insights become not only possible, but inevitable. You see and experience Hecate's realms, more so even than is known to you.

Hecate now reveals another of her aspects; the goddess of torches, surrounded by burning sconces. Her dark robes and her sombre face are lit by the orange flames. Then, with a motion of her arms, they are extinguished and fall to the ground. For a moment, in the blackness that follows, you can see nothing, but then your eyes adjust, and you see Hecate sitting among the spent torches, now the calm, veiled goddess of darkness.

And you are no longer afraid of the dark.

Hecate laughs, but not maliciously. She says, 'You sought me and have endured. Think about my different forms.'

You reflect then that her mare's face is simply a reflection of how you've sometimes held on to bad dreams in the light of day. Her dog-nature merely reflects childhood fears that held you back from choosing a path at the crossroads. Her witch-form represents your deep desires for a magical life, prevented by the fear with which you are conditioned.

Hecate says: 'Now you understand. You were bold enough to drink from my witch-cup. Surely the only potentially dangerous mask I wore was the appearance of a human woman, in the guise of witch, who offered you a cup of unknown contents. But drink you did!'

At ease and enlightened, having understood more of Hecate's true nature, you walk beside her. As you do so, you may ask her questions. You might also ask to see the future, and at this point concentrate on positive intentions, which you must show Hecate in your mind. Visualise the outcomes you want for the future strongly. After you have related all your desires, thank the goddess for that which is to come. Do not ask her for these outcomes. Imagine they have already begun happening from this moment, and that within the stream of time have already occurred.

You walk through the night, communing with the goddess, until the road gradually slopes uphill towards the rising sun. The path of the new dawn and new beginnings. By the time you reach the summit you are alone. Hecate has dissolved into the morning mist.

When you are ready to leave the pathworking, return to the garden by visualising the central tree clearly. This is your beacon and your guide. Be aware that a part of yourself remained there while you were travelling. It was and is your anchor. Return to that part of yourself simply by thinking this. You find yourself standing beneath the tree, feeling calm and refreshed. Return to normal consciousness and open your eyes.

Women as Demons

Based upon a vintage photograph

The Non-Conformists

Demons, by their very nature, seem created to vex, punish, torment or seduce and murder unsuspecting humans. They are rarely presented in a positive light. So why would anyone want to connect with them in a visualisation?

The truth is that entities regarded as demons or evil spirits are quite often deities or supernatural beings that were once regarded as benign and were only 'demonised' by a new belief system that came to usurp the older one of which these beings were a part. They are also entities that embodied what was regarded as less desirable or 'ungodly' drives and desires that can be experienced by humans.

The behaviour of a demon can be provocative, eccentric, deceitful, unconventional, irresponsible, dangerous, cruel, immodest, or unwise, as well as, of course, downright wicked. To communities or belief systems restricted and conservative in their ways, any of these behaviours, particularly in women, were therefore commonly seen as demonic. They could only be caused by evil spirits and a threat to the status quo.

However, you can connect with certain entities that embody these qualities if you simply regard them as beings who symbolise the rejection of rigid conformity. In a close-knit and close-minded community, refusal to conform is possibly one of the most courageous things a person, especially a woman, could do.

We do not recommend this approach for all demons, merely the ones explored here. In this section we have the archetypal women of the night, the succubi and seductresses who are the doom of men. But also they simply embody liberty, the freedom to be your own true self, released from the prison of small-mindedness, prudery and judgement.

Bas Relief of Lilith

Lilith
Heroine of Emancipation

> *Of Adam's first wife, Lilith, it is told*
> *(The witch he loved before the gift of Eve,)*
> *That, ere the snake's, her sweet tongue could deceive,*
> *And her enchanted hair was the first gold.*
> *And still she sits, young while the earth is old,*
> *And, subtly of herself contemplative,*
> *Draws men to watch the bright web she can weave,*
> *Till heart and body and life are in its hold.*
> *The rose and poppy are her flower; for where*
> *Is he not found, O Lilith, whom shed scent*
> *And soft-shed kisses and soft sleep shall snare?*
> *Lo! As that youth's eyes burned at thine, so went*
> *Thy spell through him, and left his straight neck bent*
> *And round his heart one strangling golden hair.*
>
> From *Lilith* by Dante Gabriel Rossetti, 1866

Lilith is thought to derive originally from the *lilītu*, a class of female demons from Mesopotamian mythology. But she is mainly known from later Jewish mythology, in which she is described as the first wife of Adam. In the ancient Hebrew language, the words *lilith* and *lilit* meant 'night creature/monster', or 'night owl'.

According to one version of the legend, Lilith was created at the same time as Adam in the Garden of Eden, and from the same soil. She was a wilful creature and refused to be subservient to Adam, even down to insisting she should be on top when they made love. He wouldn't agree to this and insisted he was superior to her, so she must go beneath him. She retorted that they had been created from the same earth, so they were equal. After this argument, Lilith went out of the Garden and met with the archangel Samael, with whom she began an affair. After this she had no desire to return to Adam or the Garden and affiliated herself to the fallen angels. She's then known as the wife of Satan (Samael).

Following this episode, Adam's next wife was created from one of his own ribs, presumably to ensure she would be more likely to toe the line.

Another version of the story goes into far more detail. It relates how Adam complained to his Creator that the woman who was supposed to be his companion had run away. God then sent out three angels, Senoy, Sansenoy and Semangelof to find her and bring her home. However, God wasn't sure the angels would succeed in their task and said to Adam that if Lilith agreed to return then everything could go back to how it was, but if not, and she wanted to remain outside of Eden, then she must agree that one hundred of her children must die every day.

The angels went in search of Lilith and eventually found her in the middle of the sea. They told her what God had said, but she still refused to return to Eden. The angels then threatened to drown her. At this, Lilith demanded that they leave her be, stating, 'I was created only to cause sickness to infants. If the infant is male, I have dominion over him for eight days after his birth, and if female, for twenty days.'

Once the angels heard this pronouncement, they were even more insistent she should return to Eden. So she suggested a compromise. If she should see a sick infant wearing an amulet that depicted the angels, or was inscribed with their names, she would have no power over that child and it would recover from its illness. She also agreed to the stipulation that one hundred of her children must die every day. This referred to the demons, which she was said to produce abundantly. The people who came after Adam made sure they wrote the angels' names on amulets they attached to sick children, safe in the knowledge that when Lilith saw the names she would remember her oath, and the children would be safe from her and survive their illnesses.

Yet another version of Lilith's story relates how she was actually created before Adam, on the fifth day. This was when God filled the waters with living creatures, and one of these was Lilith. A similar story tells how Lilith was formed from the same earth as Adam, but some time before him. The third version is even more bizarre. It describes how when God originally created Adam and Lilith, the female part was contained within the male.

When Adam was first created, a thousand evil souls attempted to take possession of him. God managed to drive them all off, but this left Adam with no soul at all and he lay as a lifeless body on the earth. God then commanded the earth to produce a living soul. Once this was created, God blew it into Adam's body with his breath. At once Adam came alive, and a female form was attached to his side. This female was Lilith. God separated the genders, and immediately Lilith flew away to the 'Cities of the Sea, and from there launched an attack on humanity.

Lilith was the first woman, so how could any humans exist for her to attack? This, of course, is simply fairy-tale logic.

Another story describes how Lilith and Samael were a combined androgynous being, as were Adam and Eve. This idea concurs with the alchemical belief that the symbolic ultimate being comprises both genders – the rebis, or sacred hermaphrodite

In the old stories, Lilith had two distinct forms. In one she's a representation of sexual desire, who leads chaste men astray, and in the other she's a murderer of children, who strangles babies in their cribs. These two aspects are separate and don't occur in the same story. She is either one or the other, almost as if she is two different characters. As witchcraft and magic became frowned upon, the child-killer aspect evolved into the dark sorceress, perhaps partial to child sacrifice.

There are so many tales of Lilith, Samael, and Adam and Eve, some of them quite strange, that it's impossible to paraphrase them all here. Suffice to say that Lilith became known as the Queen of Demons, and the Mistress of the Succubi, and was associated with witchcraft and demonology. She's seen by many modern pagans as a positive symbol for women – the first feminist, if you like, since she refused to be subservient to Adam.

Meeting Lilith

Begin the pathworking by entering the Garden of Gateways. To meet with Lilith, you will go into the eastern part of the garden.

Take the appropriate exit from the centre of the garden and follow the path to the eastern gateway, where you will seek the dawn of creation, in an airy High Place, the land of Eden.

You find yourself at the border of a wondrous garden, in the centre of which a great tree rises far into the sky. There's a sense of being very high above the earth. The four rivers of Paradise take their rise in the garden and around it is a moat of deep water, which is guarded by fierce-looking angelic beings that carry spears and swords.

You recognise this place as Eden, where humanity was created in the Judaeo-Christian belief system.

As you stand on the opposite bank of the moat, looking into the garden, you see a female figure approaching. She appears very dark, almost as if robed in swirling shadows, her long black hair streaming out behind her. You know this is Lilith, at the moment she left Eden. She seems very angry.

As she reaches the boundary, the guardians utter sounds like unearthly, booming trumpets and threaten her with their weapons. Contemptuously, she hisses at them and nimbly leaps over the moat. She notices you and comes to a standstill. 'And what do *you* want?' she asks.

You tell her why you've come, that you want to learn her mysteries. She seems to find this very amusing and tells you she's hardly a mystery, just a vexation. But she's willing to show you what she represents, what she became after leaving the garden.

She turns you into a succubus, a female demon who tempts and seduces men in their sleep. But you know that even here Lilith is being facetious, for the succubus is nothing more than a man's own desires, and if they should be repressed so they come to feel like a demon intent on destroying chastity and continence.

You fly with Lilith above the world, which spins around in myriad colours below you, history revolving, back and forth, pictures unfurling like tapestries.

Lilith shows you all the reasons why womankind has been demonised in patriarchal societies – primarily because of their sexuality and the fact that men feel helpless before it. Men are *made* to experience desire, for a sound biological reason, yet so often throughout history they have resisted this and resented it. So women had to be punished and demonised.

But this doesn't simply apply to women denigrated for their sexuality. People of all kinds are demonised constantly – judged and found wanting by others who think everyone should be like them, think like them, believe as they do. Liberty cannot thrive in circumstances ruled by judgement, dogma and restriction, whatever form it takes.

Lilith takes you into the world, where you walk unseen beside her. She shows you examples of demonising that take place every day, in small ways and in catastrophically larger ways. You're aware Lilith represents the ability to rise above such oppression, to recognise it even when it's at work within yourself, those horrible mangled opinions, thoughts and emotions that spawn bigotry and zealotry. Those who think they act for the greater good, who think they are liberators, that their opinions are the only right ones, might very well be regarded as oppressors by those they wish to convince should think as they do.

Lilith tells you: 'It's a tricky thing, freedom, for it means different things to different people. And who are you to judge? Is your way *truly* right? Or just *your* right? Are you really suited to tell people what's good for them? It's a complex issue that you could ponder all your life and never find the answer.'

You realise that Lilith's mystery, the lesson she can teach you, is to be true to yourself, and to suspend the tendency to judge others. But you're human, imperfect, and if you cannot live up to such an ideal, don't punish yourself. Just learn from your experiences. As Lilith knows only too well, we do not live in a perfect world, and it's doubtful we ever will.

Spend some time exploring these ideas, communing with Lilith, who is forever a part of yourself. Let her out, and you're not a demon but a wiser soul.

When you are ready to leave the pathworking, return to the garden by visualising the central tree clearly. This is your beacon and your guide. Be aware that a part of yourself remained there while you were travelling. It was and is your anchor. Return to that part of yourself simply by thinking this. You find yourself standing beneath the tree, feeling calm and refreshed. Return to normal consciousness and open your eyes.

Lamia by Danielle Lainton

Lamia
Beautiful Serpent

Her head was serpent, but ah, bitter-sweet!
She had a woman's mouth with all its pearls complete:
And for her eyes: what could such eyes do there
But weep, and weep, that they were born so fair?

From *Lamia* by John Keats

In ancient Greek mythology, Lamia was originally a queen of Libya, renowned for her great beauty. She was a lover of the god Zeus, who fathered several children for her. But the relationship, if such it could be termed, came with a terrible cost. Hera, Zeus's wife – who had to cope with many instances of her husband's infidelity – succumbed to her usual destructive jealousy and sought to damage her rival.

There are two versions of the story. In one, Hera simply murders all Lamia's children and transforms her into a child-eating monster, cursed to hunt children for eternity, to kill and devour them. A variant of this claims that Hera forced Lamia to devour her own children. In another version, Hera steals Lamia's offspring, causing the Libyan queen to lose her sanity through grief and despair. Such is the extent of her anguished madness, that she's driven to steal and devour other people's children, simply because she envies these parents so much and can't bear their happiness. Over time, she transformed from a mad woman into a true monster. She became a *drakaina*, a serpent or dragon that still possesses some human features. Another term for such a being is *empusa*, which is found in various Greek myths, referring to a shape-shifting female who, among her attributes, can take on the form of a snake-woman.

Lamia is sometimes described as having the head, torso and arms of a woman, but the lower parts of a snake. It's believed that this image became the most common and popular one, following the publication of John Keats' long romantic-tragedy poem 'Lamia', in which he describes her specifically as having the body of a serpent but the head of a beautiful woman. (He doesn't describe her as having a human torso or arms.) Another legend depicts her simply as a woman with a hideously-distorted face.

Modern scholars suggest her name derives from a Proto-Indo stem *-lem*, which means 'nocturnal spirit', but the ancient Greek writer Aristophanes believed her name originated from a word for 'gullet', which he proposed referred to her consumption of children.

Later versions of Lamia's story relate that Hera cursed her with the inability to close her eyes, and that she would always see the image of her dead children before them. Eventually, Zeus took pity on Lamia and gave her the ability to remove her eyes when she wished to do so. In this way, she'd be able to blank out the horrifying visions occasionally and find rest. It's said that with this gift she also gained a talent for prophecy. At the same time, Zeus granted her the ability to shape-shift.

Over time, the story of Lamia became embellished, and she was absorbed into European folklore as a monster with which to frighten children into good behaviour. She evolved into many creatures – the *lamiae*, which were like vampires and succubi combined. They were said to seduce young men and then feed upon their blood. Often in literature, Lamia – or the *lamiae* – are depicted as bloodthirsty seductresses, and the term can now mean a heartless adventuress who ruins men.

Interestingly, in some accounts, Lamia's gender is ambiguous. In two of Aristophanes' plays, he mentions

'Lamia's testicles' as foul-smelling objects. In an old bestiary, *History of Four-Footed Beasts,* by Edward Topsell, published in 1607, the *lamia* is described as having the upper body of a woman, but the hind quarters of a goat, as well as large testicles, and being covered entirely by scales.

As to what Lamia could mean to you in a spiritual sense, look at the theme behind her myths. Lamia was tormented for being beautiful. Hera chose to single her out for punishment even though the old stories inform us Zeus had sex with just about every goddess, female spirit or human woman he could get his hands on. Hera attacked Lamia in a way she thought would be the worst for any woman: to make her kill her own children. Lamia's demonisation mirrors some of Lilith's myths. She too was forced to let one hundred of her children be killed every day, so that she might live in freedom, beyond the Garden of Eden.

In reality, people are often twisted by circumstances beyond their control to become 'bad people', or at least to have episodes of being what others might call bad. We can lash out in pain, revenge, despair or outrage, which afterwards we might feel guilty or ashamed about. For a time, we were the snake-tailed monster, causing destruction, perhaps damaging relationships, working environments or social connections through an uncontrollable emotional outburst.

In the Greek myths, Lamia was demonised because of the vicious jealousy of a goddess. If people are gifted, beautiful or successful, they can incur the envious wrath of others. Lamia represents this too.

You could say that negative emotions are our children, produced by chemicals in our brains. Devouring these could be seen as a good thing, if we imagine that the act of devouring is assimilating those aspects of ourselves, understanding why they manifest and learning to control them better. Discover what the snake maiden can teach you.

Meeting Lamia

Begin the pathworking by entering the Garden of Gateways. To meet with Lamia, you will go into the southern part of the garden, seeking the element of fire, the heat which all serpents love.

Take the appropriate exit from the centre of the garden and follow the path to the southern gateway.

You emerge into a landscape at sunset. This is a hot country and the air is still very warm, even though the sun is sinking. You are walking upon a rough track through woodland. Between the trees you catch glimpses of dark pools, shrines and ruins. You become aware that this is an archetypal forest where all magical beings reside.

Now you hear a rustle in the foliage beside you and are drawn to investigate. You push aside shrubs and branches, following the sound, and emerge into a clearing.

Here there is a deep pool, behind which are dark rocks. The grass in the clearing is long and you can see it shivering, as if something is moving through it. This creature reaches the water and in the dim light you can't quite make out what it is, although it slithers into the water like a snake, leaving ripples behind it.

You approach the pool and peer into it. You can see a long sinuous shape swimming between waving weeds that look like human hair. Then you realise some of it *is* hair, and a face appears beneath the surface looking up at you. It has the features of a beautiful woman, her hair spread out around her in the water. She moves to the surface and breaks through it.

Lamia has shown herself to you, rearing up from the pool. She appears to be a human woman, but you can see that from the waist down she has the body of a serpent. She gazes at you almost wistfully, as if expecting you to judge her, to call her a monster.

You hold out your hands to her and she takes them. There is a connection between you. Visualise now all the times you've lashed out in anger or hurt.

Lamia tells you that the feelings you had at those times were poison, like the venom of a snake. She will draw this poison from you for she knows its nature.

Reflect on how we are all the serpent woman in some respect – a combination of impulses and feelings that sometimes burst out of us uncontrollably. Lamia also embodies the idea of how we can turn ideas around, from negative to positive. In legend, Lamia became a vampiric succubus who seduced her victims rather than springing a violent attack on them. This can be interpreted as using persuasion rather than rage to achieve results. Against an enemy use wiles, rather than a weapon.

In the belief systems of Malaysia and India, the half-serpent, half-human *naga* is a semi divine being that lives in caves and pools and often guards immense wealth. The *nagini*, the female of the species, might be venomous and as such a danger to humans should they incur her wrath, but she is fundamentally benign.

The offering we can give to Lamia is a new interpretation of her aspects, syncretism with a different understanding of the snake woman. This does not erase Lamia's past, merely adds an extra dimension to her.

Take some time to explore the meaning of the snake woman, what this archetype can mean to you personally, and how you can use it as a tool for evolution. Speak with Lamia, hear her words. Perhaps even take on the form of an *empusa* and see through her eyes.

When you are ready to leave the pathworking, return to the garden by visualising the central tree clearly. This is your beacon and your guide. Be aware that a part of yourself remained there while you were travelling. It was and is your anchor. Return to that part of yourself simply by thinking this. You find yourself standing beneath the tree, feeling calm and refreshed. Return to normal consciousness and open your eyes.

Lamia's Pool by Storm Constantine

Traditional illustration of Melusine

Melusine
Shape-Shifting Fairy

Once every seven years, Mélusine returns,
either as a serpent with a golden key in its mouth
or as a beautiful woman.
All it will take to win her freedom is for some brave soul
to kiss the womanly vision
or take the key from the serpent's mouth.

From an old version of the Melusine myth
from Luxembourg

Melusine is a spirit associated with sacred springs and rivers in European folklore. The most well-known story about her is found in a French fairy-tale. It's interesting that more than one noble family claim descent from Melusine, and not just in France.

The fairy-tale tells how Elynas, the King of Albany (Scotland) was hunting alone in the forest, and heard a beautiful song drifting through the trees, which sounded as if it was the ripple of cool flowing waters made into a voice. Driven to seek out she who sang, Elynas followed the sound and eventually came upon a beautiful woman. Her name was Pressyne and she was a water fairy. Elynas was smitten by her and begged her to marry him, but she would only do so if he promised he wouldn't enter her chamber while she gave birth to her children, or later while she bathed them. Elynas didn't realise Pressyne was a fairy and therefore had to live by certain taboos. After a while she gave birth to triplets, three daughters, who she named Palatyne, Melior and Melusine. Elynas was so eager to see these children that he broke his promise and entered his wife's chamber as she was bathing the babies. Distraught, but powerless to act against the laws of her kind, Pressyne left her husband, taking her children with her. She travelled to the mythical isle of Avalon.

The girls grew up happily in Avalon, but on their fifteenth birthday – symbolising perhaps the onset of womanhood – the eldest sister, Melusine, asked their mother why she'd left their father and brought them to Avalon. Pressyne kept her love for Elynas to herself, for she still grieved for him. Instead, she simply told her daughter about the broken promise, which meant Pressyne had had no choice but to leave their home. After hearing of this, Melusine vowed to take revenge. She spoke with her sisters, and behind their mother's back, they went to Albany, where they kidnapped Elynas, and took all his riches. Then they imprisoned their father within a mountain, with all his treasures beside him.

Pressyne found out what her daughters had done and was very angry. She told them they must be punished for the disrespect they had shown their father. Melusine's punishment was that every Saturday she would take on the form of a serpent (or in some versions, a fish) from the waist down.

One day, Raymond of Poitou, the adopted son of Count Emmerick of Poitou, was out hunting in the forest. He met Melusine there and at the sight of her was smitten, much as Melusine's father had been by Pressyne. He asked her to marry him, and in the tradition begun by her mother, she accepted, but on one condition. He must never enter her chamber on a Saturday. Raymond agreed to this and they were married, but as Elynas had done, he couldn't resist breaking the promise, no doubt curious as to why his wife had demanded he make it. He then saw her in her enchanted form, but Melusine was prepared to forgive him, as he still loved her, despite what he had seen. However, some time later, the pair had a quarrel, and in front of the entire court, Raymond spoke in anger, and called his wife a serpent. At this, Melusine transformed into a dragon. But she didn't cause any harm. She simply gave Raymond two magical rings and flew away, never to return.

There are several versions of this old story. In one, Melusine becomes queen of the fairies. In another it's the fact she gives birth to children who are in some way deformed or not quite human that makes Raymond denounce her. It's said that King Richard I of England used to tell a story in which he revealed that the Countess of Anjou, from whom he was descended, was in fact the fairy Melusine.

This version tells of an early Count of Anjou who, when travelling through distant lands, met a mysterious but very beautiful woman named Melusine. Despite not knowing where she came from, or who her family were, he fell in love with her, married her, and then took her to his home in Anjou. They lived quite happily, and it was only after the lady had born the Count four sons that he began to feel discomfort around her. He thought about how she didn't attend Church very often, and even when she did, she'd leave before the Mass. His suspicions overcame him and turned to paranoia. One Sunday, he ordered some of his men to restrain his wife as she made to leave the Church. Melusine, however, wouldn't be so easily caught. In front of the entire congregation, she slipped away from her would-be captors, clasped her two youngest sons to her and bore them up into the air. She flew out of the church through the highest of its stained-glass windows, no doubt shattering it as she did so. Melusine and the two boys were never seen nor heard of again, but one of the remaining sons was allegedly the ancestor of the kings of England.

Another story is believed to be an earlier version of the Melusine myth. It concerns a woman who, for some misdemeanour, was turned into a dragon by the goddess Diana. The dragon was one hundred feet long and hideous to behold. She was the mistress of a large castle, from which she emerged three times a year, and ruled over several islands. It was said that if a knight was brave enough to kiss her she would turn back into a woman. She would then make the knight her consort, who would rule with her over the islands of her domain. Many knights thought this would be an easy enough task and went to end the curse, but every one of them fled in horror and panic when they beheld the terrifying creature the lady had become. It was said they all died shortly after their cowardly flight. Unlike the tale of the Sleeping Beauty, there was never a kiss to end the curse, and the lady was doomed to a life of solitude.

Some writers equate Melusine with a water nymph, such as Lorelei, who's another fairy creature of European myth. The water nymphs are also known as nixies and are thought responsible for placing changelings among human children.

In all the stories, she's described (in her transformed aspect) as having the upper body of a woman, and the lower body of a serpent or fish. Sometimes she has two tails, and occasionally she's shown with wings.

Because of the associations with the name Melusine, it was in earlier times considered an unlucky name in some areas, and no doubt any parents who wanted to christen their child as such would be regarded with dark suspicion.

Meeting Melusine

Caroline Wise

Begin the pathworking by entering the Garden of Gateways. To meet with Melusine, you will go into the western part of the garden.

Take the appropriate exit from the centre of the garden and follow the path to the western area.

At the well-pool in the water garden, you stand gazing into the water. You become aware of the sound of a woman singing a cross between a chant and a lament. There are no discernible words, just beautiful notes that awaken something in you, a longing for beauty, for independence, and a yearning for justice.

Images appear in the well-pool, as if it is a scrying mirror. You see a great hall in an early medieval castle, with a group of nine ladies at their spinning wheels. They are French in style, wearing high pointed hats and red dresses. You become aware of the whirring sound as the wheels spin, with the lament chant weaving through it. They are concentrating on their work, but one of the ladies looks up from her wheel. She speaks, saying 'You will meet our forbear Melusine, initiator of our line, and hear her words, for women are the spinners and weavers of the tapestries of life, but few hear the messages they show of our stories. More must hear the voice in your time, for we are trapped in the role once allotted to human women, but people of your time can be free.' And the waters start to spin too...

The exquisite chant grows louder, and suddenly ceases. From this whirlpool, a naked woman with small wings rises from the water. She reminds you of the mythical siren – the supernatural winged woman who seduces men at sea with her beautiful song, and drags them, without mercy, to a watery grave. They would lash themselves to the ship's mast so as not to succumb to her alluring charms. You feel no such fear, being curiously upbeat and intrigued.

Melusine takes your hand and pulls you down into the spring. The water is clear and cold, and you find you can breathe and see clearly. It is exhilarating, as she dives onwards in this deep cold water. The sides are a stark rocky sheath that is covered in dark green water weed. Your feet move as a diver's, your hair streams out behind you. Now you emerge into a wide circular underground lake. Fish pass by. There are bones on the floor, and silver coins, and tall tapering water plants dance in the movement of the water. There are nine underwater arches that lead off from the circular wall. At each sits a shadowy female figure hunched over a spinning wheel, spinning waterweed into yarn. Closer inspection shows these to be old, thin, non-human beings, with spindly arms and fingers and legs. They are concentrating on their work, but one looks up at you and speaks. She says, 'If they knew how bad this yarn tastes on the lips, if they know how sharp this yarn cuts the wrists, if they knew how they cannot break the bonds of our yarn, would that stop them?' You have no idea what the grim words mean, but they cause a stirring inside you.

Melusine now tells you that her waters feed the underground streams, through these arches, which in turn branch off into myriad streams which burst forth at the sites known to humankind as holy wells. She explains that these are the wormholes of harsh reality and clarity. The underground streams have been a symbol for the lost wisdom of the goddess for millennia, and in times when the severe religions of men drove Her underground,

Melusine and her kind have warded Her safe passage towards those who are receptive.

Melusine says to you: 'I am of fairy, between the worlds of men and beasts and gods, and I guard Her kin within your realm. My silent companions are spinning out the lot of those who transgress. You will learn of this.

'I was human once – I was enchanted and cast into the well, and my spirit found affinity with the cold water and the weeds. I sang my song, so I did not forget my soul, and to attract those who may need to hear my voice. I am cast as a demon, because the truth is too uncomfortable. A demon, yet aristocrats fight to claim descent from me, as I am grander than their noble forbears! How pathetic are most of your kind to my eyes. Let me reveal my dragon nature to you.'

You notice that her mermaid's tail has become as a mighty serpent. Green scales glint as it swishes. Her upper body is of a winged dragon, her voice now sibilant through pointed teeth.

'But you, you have sought me, some part of you was waiting for this encounter. You want to know me, not to claim an exotic lineage, or steal my power or violate me. Therefore, you are truly of my clan, of the Line that runs Deep. You wish to know my nature, not steal it, so I will awaken it in you. I offer you this:

'Invoke me should any seek to defile you, your family, your children or your friends; when someone's gaze is awry, when their nature is predatory. I will drag them down and trap their spirit in the thick black mud. With my fey-sisters' yarn of slimy weed, I will bind them here as a five-fold punishment – of the feet, the genitals, the hands and the throat and the lips. I will strip them of their riches, I will coil around them with my serpent form. I will hunt them down through my labyrinth of subterranean streams. I am the shape-shifting Fey, the Fairy Queen, protector of women, children and the vulnerable, the Dragon in the depths of the subconscious mind.

'In time of need, remember me: call forth the coiled serpent, your fairy self, your dragon power, and I will arise. For I am in you: you can be all of these.'

You gasp in awe and respect and gratitude and see Melusine is now once more in her winged mermaid form. She grabs your hand again, and with one dynamic thrust, she rises upwards and you break through the surface of the spring. You are alone as you scramble out. You mull over what she has told you, and how she claimed you as her clan, of how she has revealed to you an aspect of inner strength deep in you, and how she has your back. Give thanks to her and cast a silver coin into the well.

Return to the garden by visualising the central tree clearly. This is your beacon and your guide. Be aware that a part of yourself remained there while you were travelling. It was and is your anchor. Return to that part of yourself simply by thinking this. You find yourself standing beneath the tree, feeling calm and refreshed. Return to normal consciousness and open your eyes.

Melusine's Fountain in the Forest by Storm Constantine

Agrat bat Mahlat by Danielle Lainton

Agrat bat Mahlat
Daughter of Lilith

'Men who fear demons see demons everywhere.'

from *The Child Thief* by Brom

Agrat bat Mahlat is a demoness from Jewish mythology. '*Bat*' means 'daughter of' so her name is Agrat, daughter of Mahlat. However, it's been suggested by scholars that Mahlat can be translated as 'illusion' or 'reward for deception'. Therefore, some modern pagans refer to her as Agrat, Daughter of Illusion.

According to an early version of the Kabbalah, Agrat is one of the four angels of sacred prostitution, whose divine function was to relieve men of their lust and purify them, so that they could not become possessed by evil spirits. Later, these angels were demonised by new religions and became succubi, creatures to be feared.

Agrat was then transformed into one of the succubi, along with her sisters Naamah and Eisheth Zenunim, who had also initially been regarded as angels of sacred prostitution. Lilith, the queen of succubi, is held to be either the mother of the three, or their grandmother. Agrat and her sisters can be regarded as manifestations of Lilith, known as the *Lilitu*. Eventually Agrat became known as a queen of demons.

Like her mother, Agrat was said to have lain with the fallen archangel Samael, who in the Judaic tradition is an angel of death, or the real name of Satan – Satan being essentially a title: 'the accuser'. The literal meaning of his name is 'venom of god'. He has been equated with Azazel, the leader of the fallen angels, but there are no definite sources to confirm this. Azazel might well be a composite of several mythological figures. Both Naamah and Eisheth were believed to be lovers of Samael.

Agrat was said to ride through the air in a chariot drawn by a bull. On the eves of Wednesday and Saturday, she became the 'dancing roof-demon', accompanied by a train of spirit messengers or angels of destruction. In this form, she dances across the roof tops, attended by her unearthly followers, while Lilith sings in a howling voice.

Agrat was also given the role of mentor and teacher, in that she was said to have imparted the secrets of magic to a Jewish wise man named Amemar. In this role, she is known as 'Mistress of the Sorceresses'. Her power over humanity was said to have been curbed by the 'spiritual intervention' of two men, Hanina ben Dosa and Rabbi Abaye.

According to one myth, Agrat was the leader of the spirits with whom the wise King Solomon communicated. They were eventually trapped inside a lamp or a similar vessel and hidden inside a cave within the cliffs around the Dead Sea. The legend goes that eventually King David discovered this lamp and released the occupants. He was taken with Agrat, who could appear to be the most beautiful of women and became intimate with her. She fell pregnant and bore a son, who was Asmodeus, a 'cambion' child, meaning he was half succubus and half human. He eventually became a king of demons. Other old stories suggest that King David fathered other demon sons, although these tales are not widely accepted within the Jewish tradition.

We can view Agrat as a playful demon, an entity who scorns convention and epitomises the joy of freedom, the freedom to behave like an irresponsible teenager with no thought of the future. We can indulge this impulse occasionally and cavort with Agrat on the roof tops.

Meeting Agrat bat Mahlat

Begin the pathworking by entering the Garden of Gateways. To meet with Agrat bat Mahlat, you will go into the eastern part of the garden.

Take the appropriate exit from the centre of the garden and follow the path to the eastern gateway, seeking Agrat as a being of Air.

You emerge upon a wide road that leads to an immense walled city of the ancient Middle East. The sun is slowly sinking and, as you approach the city, bats fly out from crannies in the towering walls.

You begin your journey to Agrat bat Mahlat by mounting stone steps set into the walls that lead up a dark passage-way to a wide fortified pathway, where robed guardians of the city patrol, armed with spears and on the alert for enemies.

You're here because you seek the roof tops of this unnamed city, for it is in this spot that Agrat and her retinue will gather this night.

The guards don't notice you as you walk the battlements of the city walls. As dusk draws on, you hear strange cries that resolve into ululating voices raised in song. It sounds like the calls of animals and birds, the hum and chitter of insects. This unearthly music swirls around you, as if beckoning you onwards.

You come to a place where you can jump onto the roof of a house and see that from here you can traverse the high points of the city. People might move below, but they don't look up. They can't perceive who and what gathers above them.

You can see shadowy shapes flickering around the city heights, which appear winged. You cross the roof tops towards them and eventually reach the roof garden of a large building. Here, Agrat is holding court. She's a beautiful, dark-skinned woman, with wild black hair. She has the legs of a goat – not hairy like a satyr, but smooth-skinned. Her strangely-jointed legs end in dainty black hooves. Enormous bat-like wings sprout from her shoulder-blades. In form, she imitates how people imagine a succubus to look. Agrat sprawls luxuriously upon cushions of silk, surrounded by her fellow succubi. They drink wine and laugh and talk together.

Agrat sees you and beckons for you to come to her. She tells you that you may join her for the evening's revels, and that she and her succubi will fly across the city, invading the dreams of those who sleep, bringing ecstasy, forbidden pleasures and release from the drudgery of life.

She offers you a cup of wine and you drink. It is a strange concoction, and you're not really sure what you're swallowing, but it warms you within. You feel dizzy for a moment, and then realise you're changing form. Like the succubi, you have leathery wings and take to the air, surrounded by the others, who are chattering and laughing together.

Agrat leads the way in a wild flight across the city. You peer into bed-chambers and can see the dreams of the sleepers. Some people are weighed down by problems and insecurities. You can relieve their cares for a while by sending them a dream full of life, desire, joy and luxury. People who are trapped may dream of liberty. People who are incapacitated by illness or age may dream of the freedoms of youth and perfect health. People who are full of rage may dream of walking from the prison of their anger. All may dream of love and desire, of meeting with their idea of the perfect lover.

This, Agrat tells you, is why she is seen as a demon. To her kind, desire is never a sin, but for some, hampered by repressive beliefs, to be true to your human nature is evil and to be conquered and banished from the heart and soul. Agrat sees this as imprisonment, unnatural, and only those who are afraid of the ecstasy of freedom see her as a demon.

For this night, you too can share the experiences of the sleepers. On some far roof top beneath the stars there may be a lover for you – your idealised, perfect mate. For fleeting hours you may enjoy their company, free of all restraint and fear.

When dawn begins to redden the eastern horizon, you find yourself alone, back in your ordinary shape, but the pleasures of the night still warm your heart.

You hear faint cries of farewell from the succubi, which changes into the call of birds as the morning wakes them. For a moment, you feel wistful for the night of abandon that's now finished, but then you remember can revisit Agrat's roof top court whenever you please.

When you are ready to leave the pathworking, return to the garden by visualising the central tree clearly. This is your beacon and your guide. Be aware that a part of yourself remained there while you were travelling. It was and is your anchor. Return to that part of yourself simply by thinking this. You find yourself standing beneath the tree, feeling calm and refreshed. Return to normal consciousness and open your eyes.

Queens of Death

The Graveyard Sentinel by Storm Constantine

In Graveyards and Underworlds

While many gods and goddesses have links with death, the afterlife and getting to the afterlife, including the Underworld and graveyards, sometimes these associations are simply qualities of a greater purpose and function. Some entities, however, are focused entirely upon death and its environments and consequences.

There are many different versions of the Underworld – some more uncomfortable places than others: a land of peace and tranquillity, the asphodel fields, the summerlands, paradise – or a swamp of ill-smelling mists, a barren place of lifeless trees, or a hell of torment, populated by salivating demons eager to inflict torture.

So why would we wish to encounter the goddesses of the Underworld? What can they teach us other than the inevitability of death?

Another recurring motif in myth and fairy stories is that of the human who ventures into the Underworld and escapes it, sometimes bringing home with them a dead loved one, who they've snatched from the rulers of the dead. So, in this sense, and particularly in our modern age, death goddesses are also goddesses of rebirth and initiation. A spiritual experience of death, an imagined extinction and the subsequent resurrection into a second life, is often a component of magical initiation, during which the initiate transcends ordinary existence and emerges from their trial a wiser and more powerful person.

In this section you'll find four female entities who embody different aspects of death and the afterlife. Approach them to learn of spiritual rebirth and how to transcend an ordinary existence into a life of magic and self-evolution.

Akhlys by Storm Constantine

Akhlys
The Mist of Death

'And beside them [the Keres (Deaths) and the Moirai (Fates)] on the battlefield, was standing Akhlys, dismal and dejected, green and pale, dirty-dry, fallen in on herself with hunger, knee-swollen, and the nails grown long on her hands. And from her nostrils the drip kept running, and from her cheeks the blood dribbled to the ground. And she stood there, grinning forever. And the dust that had gathered and lay in heaps on her shoulders was muddy with tears.'

Hesiod

Akhlys, (also known as Achlys), is a goddess of ancient Greece, and is perhaps one of the most fearsome to imagine. She represents the 'mist of death' that clouds the eyes preceding death, and her name literally means 'misted eyes'.

She is described by Hesiod as being a personification of misery and sadness. In appearance, she is pale and emaciated, eternally weeping. Her teeth chatter and her fingernails are abnormally long. Her knees are swollen and her cheeks bloody, while her shoulders are covered thickly with dust. Hardly an attractive figure to come across in a dark and lonely spot.

In an account by Nonnus, she provides poison for the goddess Hera, which effects a hideous transformation on those who have displeased Hera:

'Hera, who turns her all-seeing eye to every place, saw from on high the everchanging shape of Lyaios [Dionysos], and knew all. Then she was angry with the

> *guardians of Bromios. She procured from Thessalian Akhlys treacherous flowers of the field and shed a sleep of enchantment over their heads. She distilled poisoned drugs over their hair. She smeared a subtle magical ointment over their faces and changed their human shape. Then they took the form of a creature with long ears, and a horse's tail that stuck out straight from the loins and flogged the flanks of its shaggy-crested owner. From the temples, a cow's horns sprouted out. Their eyes widened under the horned forehead. Their hair ran across their heads in tufts. Long white teeth grew out of their jaws. A strange kind of mane grew, covering their necks with rough hair, and which ran down from the loins to underneath the feet.'*
>
> *Dionysiaca* by Nonnus (trans. Rouse)
> Greek epic 5th century AD

Akhlys is also, according to some ancient myths, a primordial goddess, a personification of eternal night, who existed even before Chaos came into being. As far as her family is concerned, although no surviving story specifies this directly, it's thought she was most likely a daughter of Nyx and therefore was one of the Keres. These were female spirits of death and doom, known in Latin as the Tenebrae (meaning Darknesses), and were the children of Nyx and Erebus, the latter being a personification of deep darkness and shadow. The Keres were fearsome spirits, with a thirst for human blood, who haunted battlefields, searching for those who were wounded or dying, and preying upon them.

From *The Shield of Herakles*:

> *'The black Dooms, gnashing their white teeth, grim-eyed, fierce, bloody and terrifying, fought over the men who were dying, for they all longed to drink dark blood. As soon as they caught a man who had fallen or was newly*

wounded, one of them clasped her great claws around him and his soul went down to Hades, to chilly Tartarus. And when they had satisfied their hearts with human blood, they would throw that one behind them, and rush back again into the battle and the tumult.'

The Keres then represent the dark energy around conflict, a mindless thirst for blood and destruction. Akhlys, however, specifically appears to haunt battlefields rather than actively feed upon the victims of war. She is a personification of the horrors of war, and also the grief that comes with them. She represents the famine and pestilence that can ravage war-torn lands. She walks the battlefield, grieving, yet leering, a hideous yet pitiful figure, starving and sick.

As for how we can relate to such a terrible goddess in our modern world, we have only to look around us, at the devastation of war in all its forms. Akhlys still walks, eternally weeping, eternally damaged, yet we can look upon her in a more positive light. We can give her the role of 'war eater' in that she clears the horrors of it, takes them into herself. She may find peace in the realm of night and shadow, her parents, and there disgorge the atrocities she has consumed. In facing Akhlys we face our fears of war and its terrible consequences.

Meeting Akhlys

Begin the pathworking by entering the Garden of Gateways. To meet with Akhlys, you will go into the southern part of the garden, seeking the element of Fire, with which a variety of war gods are associated.

Take the appropriate exit from the centre of the garden and follow the path to the southern area.

On leaving the garden, you emerge in an area ravaged by martial conflict. Buildings lie in ruins, refugees huddle by the roadsides. Vehicles of war rumble across the raddled landscape. You hear the stutter of gunfire, the dull boom of explosions. The air is full of smoke and dust and the smell of death. It seems to you that the only creatures who gain from this horror are the carrion eaters.

This could be any country, for nearly every land in our world has at one time been ravaged by war.

Tentatively, you walk into the ruins, terrified of what you might see. There are indeed countless bodies lying around and there are people grieving for the dead. You're aware of their inconsolable misery at the waste of human life, of those they love. These people have lost everything. Their community is shattered, their homes reduced to dust. Why are humankind so aggressive, so heartless and cruel? It's unbearable to you.

Soon, you too are weeping at this senseless destruction. You're almost staggering through the sprawling battlefield.

Then, ahead, you see a strange sight: the figure of a woman in the centre of the carnage. She is hideously thin, clad in ragged robes and shawl. You can see the fingernails on her skeletal hands are unnaturally long and jagged. She is weeping; her withered, blood-stained face hardly more than a skull.

You know this is Akhlys, known as the Mist of Death, and that you must approach her, for this is why you are here. As you draw closer you see that her eyes are milky, misty as if with cataracts.

She says to you: 'I am the reflection of the evil humankind can do to one another. I absorb the horrors of your wars. This is my face. I carry the wounds and grief of all. I am the sorrow wept by mothers, wives, sisters and daughters. I am the fear felt by fathers, husbands, brothers and sons. I am the outcome and consequences of brutality.'

The scene shifts before you and you're given glimpses of times of conflict throughout human history, from the very earliest times. This horror has always been with us, even if the means to damage and destroy one another has become more sophisticated over time.

Akhlys shows you that wars are caused by fear or greed – either the fear of another nation, or a gang, or a tribe, or even a single person (wars can be small as well as great), or the greed of wanting something that someone else has got.

Then, the scenes shift again, and you see into your own life, the small, petty wars in which you have fought, and lost or won. You see grievance that can grow into fury and the desire to attack.

Akhlys's lesson, as it applies to us, is that we must transcend such destructive, base instincts. We might not be able to change the bigger picture, but we can certainly change our own small part in the world. This, as an inhabitant of our planet, is often the best we can do.

As you're contemplating these things you become aware that occasionally the decision to go to war might be taken because there is no other way to deal with an aggressor, and the action in that sense is defence. Those who threaten others weaker or more vulnerable than themselves might be implacable, ruthless and without compassion. The decision to fight fire with fire is ugly. It can be a complex matter. But the outcome is the same. Victories, in some senses, are always hollow and come with a terrible price.

Akhlys says to you she absorbs it all, takes the wounds upon her own body. She says:

'When anger controls you, and the desire to strike out, think of me. For this is a little war. When you see the grief of families, torn apart by combat in the countries of the world, call upon me to go to them. For this is the greater war. I am she who walks the aftermath of conflict, who weeps for the dead and those who are injured and in mourning. I am the mist of death in the warriors' eyes.'

This seems so terrible a thing, you're overcome with compassion for this tortured goddess. You ask her what you might do for her to relieve her pain.

At this she manages a wan smile and says: 'As long as there is compassion and love in the hearts of humankind, there is hope. When hurts are healed, at any level, then so my hurts heal too. Work for the day when I no longer walk and can find my peace in the lands below. This is your duty as a child of earth.'

She asks that now, before you leave, you visualise with her a world free of war, a time of peace, when she will vanish into the mist.

When you are ready to leave the pathworking, return to the garden by visualising the central tree clearly. This is your beacon and your guide. Be aware that a part of yourself remained there while you were travelling. It was and is your anchor. Return to that part of yourself simply by thinking this. You find yourself standing beneath the tree, feeling calm and refreshed. Return to normal consciousness and open your eyes.

The Realm of War by Storm Constantine

Dea Tacita by Storm Constantine

Dea Tacita
She of the Silence

See, an old woman, full of years, sitting in the middle of the girls, performs rites to Dea Tacita, yet is anything but tacit herself; and places, with three fingers, three stalks of frankincense under the threshold, where the lowly mouse has made itself a secret passage. She then binds together enchanted threads with a dark reel, and rolls in her mouth seven black beans. And after sealing a *pilcher's head with pitch, and piercing it with a needle of brass, she stitches it up, and roasts it in the fire. She also drops wine on it, and whatever wine is left either she drinks herself, or her attendants do, but herself the greater portion. 'The tongue of the foe we have tied up, and the mouths of our enemies,' says she, departing; and the old woman makes her exit staggering drunk.

'Fasti', Part 1, Book Two, by Ovid
(Translated by William Thynne, 1833)

(*The archaic meaning for pilcher is 'scabbard', or a covering for a sword, but at least one analysis of this passage suggests the pilcher is a fish-head.)

While little is known about this Roman goddess, she's an interesting character. Her name means 'the silent goddess', and she was a deity of the dead, inhabiting an eerie marsh in the Underworld.

The concept of silence can be interpreted various ways. She is the silence of the tomb, the silence of the lightless Underworld, but also silence in the living world – that of a sealed mouth, a still tongue.

The Roman poet Ovid, wrote about this goddess in his *'Fasti'*, an excerpt of which is at the head of this page. The excerpt describes a rite to propitiate Dea Tacita, so that 'hostile mouths and unfriendly tongues' will be silenced. Dea Tacita is in fact more like an epithet than a name, and there is a Roman myth that relates to this idea, and the fact that the title was *given*. Ovid tells this story very shortly after describing the silencing rite.

According to the legend, the highest of the gods, Jupiter, lusted after a goddess of springs, fountains and wells named Juturna. Eventually, he turned her into a water nymph, or naiad and gave her several sacred wells over which to preside. But before that she spurned his advances, often diving into the waters of a river to escape him. Jupiter called together all the water goddesses and naiads of the area, and persuaded, or rather ordered, them to help him. They must prevent their sister from getting away from him. This they vowed do to. But one of the nymphs named Larunda (or Lara), who was renowned for being gossipy and indiscreet, warned Juturna not to go near the banks of the river, and revealed all that Jupiter had said. Larunda also went to Juno, Jupiter's wife, and told her all that was going on or, as the 19th century translator William Thynne describes it: 'that husband of yours is wenching after the naiad Juturna'.

When Jupiter heard of this betrayal, he cut out Larunda's tongue, and told the god Mercury: 'Lead her to the shades below – proper place that for the still. She shall be a water goddess, but it shall be of an infernal marsh.'

Larunda was sent to a gloomy Underworld location, and here became associated with the dead. We can imagine the stagnant waters of this dismal spot, the blackened trees, the lowering sky, the lifeforce held in stasis, and the utter silence.

Upon the journey to this dire place, Mercury himself

was smitten by Larunda's beauty and forced himself upon her. The story goes that Larunda could not plead with him to spare her, as she could make no sound. She could only speak with her eyes, but this could not prevent her fate. Subsequently, she gave birth to twins, who Ovid believed became the spirits known as the Lares. They became guardian deities, who protected the home and all within its boundaries. Statues of them would be placed upon dining-tables, and would be present to bless ceremonies, such as marriages.

While remembered mainly as household gods or goddesses, the Lares did in fact have wider influence, and were believed also to protect livestock, fields, roads and boundaries. In one version of the tale, the twins – who were boys – were as silent as their mother was, and could be referred to as the *taciti manes*, or spirits of silence.

Some writers claim that once Larunda's tongue was removed, she was known as Dea Muta, the goddess deprived of speech, and it was only once she arrived in the Underworld she became Dea Tacita. It seems credible that Larunda *is* the Dea Tacita, the silent goddess called upon to seal up mouths and end gossip or libel.

There are several festival days associated with Dea Tacita. Feralia, celebrated on 21st February, is connected with the Manes, or the souls of dead loved ones. Families would make offerings to their ancestors at this time, and it was a propitious day for Dea Tacita to be called upon to silence enemies. The next day, the 22nd, was the Caristia, and this was a time when people cast off the gloom they might have felt the day before, while contemplating death and the dead. At this time, they focused upon all their loved ones who were still in the land of the living.

In her guise of Larunda, Dea Tacita was venerated on 23rd December at a festival named the Larentalia.

One interpretation of the silent goddess is that she is a personification of the terror of obscurity. Fundamentally, this means the fear of not being heard or seen, and that in itself can mean many things. Dea Tacita has also been described as a muse, and one legend tells that Numa Pompilius, the second king of Rome, believed she granted him the ability to be an oracle.

While Dea Tacita is the silence of death, death can take many forms. It is seen as an ending or a transformation. We can see that silence is often useful and beneficial – the tongue that does not wag doesn't cause hurt or ruin lives. Dea Tacita can teach us when to be silent.

One of the tenets of modern witchcraft is the saying: 'to know, to dare, to will and to be silent'. We do not have to brag about our accomplishments. If we are secure in ourselves, proud of our achievements without being vain or vainglorious, we are happier people. A true mage does not have to have power over others; they seek power over only themselves. They keep their own counsel.

But also, as illustrated in Larunda's myth, sometimes it's best *not* to keep silent. Larunda could not speak of the violation Mercury forced upon her. If we see or learn of something bad happening, but are worried about the consequences of speaking out, Dea Tacita can help impart the wisdom to know when it is right to do so.

Meeting Dea Tacita

Begin the pathworking by entering the Garden of Gateways. To meet with Dea Tacita, you will go into the northern part of the garden.

Take the appropriate exit from the centre of the garden and follow the path to the north.

As before in this direction, the path leads you to a cave, but this time as you approach it the vegetation around you begins to change. The light is dim and greenish, the trees stand drooping and lifeless in a stagnant mire, surrounded by tall dead reeds and grasses. You can't hear the call of birds.

Once you enter the cave, the atmosphere is dank and unpleasant, and the roof very low so you have to stoop uncomfortably to continue your journey.

Groping your way in the dark, you eventually emerge into a brooding landscape of swampland. Here the air is misty, and all colours are dulled; muted greens, browns, duns and sickly yellow.

You follow a path of wooden planks that has been constructed over the treacherous ground, and occasionally torches stand on rough poles to light the way. The only sounds you hear are the strange croakings of amphibians, but *are* they only toads and frogs? Large bodies seem to slither through the reedy pools. Occasionally, you hear the screech of some kind of carrion bird. But the further you walk, so the sounds die away into utter, deathly silence. You find you want to hold your breath because even your breathing sounds too loud to you.

Presently, up ahead, you see a stone building through the moss-hung trees. A side path veers off towards it and you are drawn to follow it. You find yourself at what seems to be a forgotten shrine. It is small and simple, yet the only offerings laid on the cracked altar are withered and rotted – dead flowers, bones and desiccated fruit.

A figure appears from between the shadows of broken columns. She is shrouded in colourless, torn robes.

'Who seeks the silence?' she asks, but the voice is in your head, rather than heard through your ears.

You know this is Larunda, who is also Dea Tacita, but

here before you in her most sorrowful aspect. This is the forlorn creature whose tongue was cut out, who could not protest her violation at the hands of a god.

You tell Larunda you are here to learn her Mysteries, and she says to you, 'Child, first learn to free your voice.'

She bids you to stand beside her at the edge of a still pool. Its surface looks oily, the waters beneath murky.

'Scry here,' Larunda whispers in your mind. 'Learn when the voice must speak.'

Now spend some minutes gazing into the water, examining all the times when to be mute isn't the best course. Sometimes we must stand up and speak for what is right. But what about costs? Might sometimes the cost of such honesty be too severe? Contemplate these matters at Larunda's side as you scry.

Eventually, you stand straight and say to Larunda, 'Bring forth Dea Tacita, to grant me the wisdom of both silence and sound.'

Larunda bows and before your eyes it's as if an older, taller woman walks through Larunda yet becomes her. She looks stern, but strong. 'I am the goddess of silence,' she says, but this time aloud. 'What do you seek in my realm?'

You ask the goddess to reveal her Mysteries to you, the knowledge of wise silence, the ability also to know when silence is not appropriate.

Dea Tacita assents, and gestures for you to walk with her through the silent realm of the dead. There is no one around, alive or otherwise, yet now you see faint glows between the trees that look like portals. You see they are misty windows revealing scenes and situations.

Through these, Dea Tacita shows the consequences of not being silent inappropriately. You see images of gossips destroying relationships, poisonous words dripped into people's ears that causes anger and violence, words that can sow the seeds of paranoia, suspicion and fear. Words that ruin lives. All these small deaths.

You say to Dea Tacita, 'Lady of Silence, I ask that you bestow upon me the wisdom to know when to speak and when to be silent.'

She tells you to contemplate situations in your life when this matter was of great importance. What action did you take? Was it for the best? Is it sometimes better to cause upset for a greater good – or not? When do you know what is for the best?

When you have finished your contemplation, Dea Tacita murmurs that only through experience will you learn, and sometimes you might make the wrong decision, but if you are truly wise you will not make the same mistake twice. Thank the goddess for all she's taught you and bid her farewell.

When you are ready to leave the pathworking, return to the garden by visualising the central tree clearly. This is your beacon and your guide. Be aware that a part of yourself remained there while you were travelling. It was and is your anchor. Return to that part of yourself simply by thinking this. You find yourself standing beneath the tree, feeling calm and refreshed. Return to normal consciousness and open your eyes.

Ereshkigal by Danielle Lainton

Ereshkigal
Queen of Irkalla

Neti, the chief doorman of the Underworld, entered the house of Ereshkigal and said: 'My mistress, there is a lone girl outside. It is Inanna, your sister, and she has arrived at the palace Ganzir.'

Ereshkigal bit her lip and took the words to heart. She said, 'Come Neti, my chief doorman of the Underworld, don't neglect the instructions I will give you. Let the seven gates of the Underworld be bolted. Then let each door of the palace Ganzir be opened separately. As for her, after she has entered, and crouched down and had her clothes removed, they will be carried away.'

Adapted from an ancient Mesopotamian text.

In Sumerian mythology, Ereshkigal was the older sister of the goddess Inanna, and features as a major character in 'The Descent of Inanna', a story/hymn that describes the goddess's descent into the Underworld, the realm of her dark sister.

The Babylonian version of this myth involves the goddess Ishtar, but is essentially the same story, featuring the same goddesses. Ereshkigal and Inanna represent the Underworld and the heavens respectively, with Inanna also presiding over political power, as well as fertility, love and beauty.

Ereshkigal was known to have had four husbands. The first was Gugulana, known as the Great Bull of Heaven, with whom she had a son, Ninazu. The goddess's sister Inanna was instrumental in the death of Gugulana. She had tried to seduce the hero Gilgamesh, who remained immune to her allure, and seeking vengeance for this affront, Inanna sent the Bull of Heaven to punish Gilgamesh. Gugulana was eventually vanquished and killed by Gilgamesh's close friend, Enkidu. This episode quite understandably damaged the relationship between the sisters. Ereshkigal's second husband was Enlil, with whom she had a son, Namtar. With a third consort, Ereshkigal had a daughter named Nungal. Her fourth consort was the plague god, Nergal. She acquired this husband in rather an unusual way.

The legend goes that a great banquet was held in the realm of the Sumerian deities, to which all gods and goddesses were invited – except for one. Ereshkigal, being queen of the Underworld, could not rise from her realm to attend. However, the gods told her that she could send an envoy in her place as a formal representative, and she chose her son and close advisor, Namtar. The gods and goddesses treated this envoy of the Underworld with the greatest respect as an equal, except for Nergal, who insulted the dark queen's representative. The other gods and goddesses were so angry at this they punished Nergal by banishing him to the realm controlled by the goddess he had disrespected by proxy. Eventually, Nergal and Ereshkigal became husband and wife, although the actual details of how their relationship developed into marriage is unknown. As a god who brought death to humanity, it was no doubt seen as fitting he became consort of the supreme goddess of death. In essence, he helped fill her domain with souls.

The Underworld in Mesopotamian mythology was known as Irkalla, and in the same way that the Greek god Hades lends his name to his realm, Ereshkigal was often referred to as Irkalla. The name Ereshkigal means 'Queen of the Great Earth'. She was also sometimes known as Ninkigal, which meant 'Lady of the Great Earth'. Additionally, she was sometimes known as Allatu, or was closely associated with another Underworld goddess of that name.

As to how Ereshkigal became queen of the dead, a story is told in the Sumerian epic poem *'Gilgamesh'*. In this version of her history, Ereshkigal was abducted by a mysterious creature called the Kur. (Kur was also an ancient name for the Underworld itself.) The Kur was known as the first dragon, and is perhaps associated with Tiamat, an important goddess in Babylonian myth, who was also referred to as a dragon. At the Kur's command, Ereshkigal was forced against her will to become the Queen of the Dead and rule over these souls in their lightless land. Even though her father Enki, the god of water, sought to avenge Ereshkigal, and apparently won a battle against the Kur, the dark queen never rose from her realm to escape her fate. She can be regarded then, as a similar goddess to Persephone, the Greek goddess abducted and taken to the Underworld by Hades. Another name for the Kur is Kurnugia, which means 'the Land of No Return'. It was said to lie in the west, beneath the Mountains of Sunset, and was a dreadful, gloomy realm, where the dead had to drink from muddy pools and had only dust to eat. In this dark country, Ereshkigal lived in a palace named Ganzir, and here ruled over the souls of the dead.

Ereshkigal is best known for her part in 'The Descent of Inanna'. Inanna, in all versions of her myths, is presented as an impulsive and ambitious goddess. She once sought to extend her power into the Underworld and took it upon herself to descend into her sister's realm, ostensibly to attend the funeral of Gugulana, for whose death she was ultimately responsible. Ereshkigal's loyal attendant Neti informed the goddess of her sister's arrival at the gates of Irkalla. Ereshkigal was far from pleased to hear this and told Neti to inform Inanna she must pass through seven gates, and at each gate must remove an article of clothing – or specifically one of the *me*, the items that comprised symbols of her power. By the time Inanna reached Ereshkigal's throne, she was naked. She was then tried by the Annunaki, seven judges of Irkalla, and found to be in the wrong. The goddess was killed instantly, and her body hung upon a hook in Ereshkigal's palace, in a place where anyone could see it.

Inanna was later rescued, due to the intervention of her close friend Ninshubur, who pleaded Inanna's case with the god Enki. The god sent two genderless beings to Irkalla to revive Inanna with the waters and food of life and to escort her home. However, a horde of angry demons, denizens of Irkalla sent by Ereshkigal, pursued Inanna. They demanded that another should be sent back down to Irkalla in her place. Upon discovering her husband, Dumuzi, had not mourned her loss sufficiently, Inanna gladly sent him as a replacement.

While Ereshkigal was feared she was also greatly respected, and in some ways regarded as of better character than her rather selfish heavenly sister.

As to how we can interact with this fearsome goddess today, she represents the process of initiation. When you replicate the descent of Inanna in visualisation, removing items that represent your 'power' along the way, your journey ends in the land of the dead, and a symbolic death/rebirth experience. In many magical and spiritual traditions, this kind of visualised rite of passage, in some cultures aided by hallucinogenic substances, is an essential component of magical or shamanic training. The idea of undergoing a trial and facing death, even in visualised form, is regarded as a path to knowledge and self-awareness.

For this meeting, you will take the shadowed, lonely path to the Underworld and face the dark goddess with courage, naked of all defences and disguises.

Meeting Ereshkigal

Begin the pathworking by entering the Garden of Gateways. To meet with Ereshkigal, you will go into the northern part of the garden. Take the appropriate exit from the centre of the garden and follow the path to the north.
You are adorned with seven items of clothing and jewellery that represent the *me* of Inanna and are your 'glamours' – the talismans that represent your earthly powers and attributes, and also the shields and defences you developed in early life through conditioning, which might hold you back from growth and self-evolution. For Inanna the *me* were a shawl, a crown, a necklace, sandals, a bracelet, earrings and an ornate belt. Become aware of these symbols of power and how they appear upon your own body.

You enter the cave in the north, surrounded by an oppressive sense of desolation. When you emerge from the rocky passageway, you find yourself in a dark and forbidding landscape. Before you, an immense range of black mountains is silhouetted against the night sky. At the feet of the Mountains of Sunset you will find the entrance to Irkalla. There is no moonlight; the sky overhead is like matte black velvet. There is no sign of life. What vegetation and trees exist are blackened and twisted, sometimes appearing horribly suggestive of petrified creatures, frozen in weird postures. The angles of the landscape and the looming crags ahead all seem wrong, which makes your head ache.
    Soon, travelling swiftly through this surreal environment, you reach the foothills of the mountains and venture into a dark chasm.
    Sheer black walls of obsidian rise to either side of you.

You follow the path, which curves round in a large spiral. Eventually, the path becomes an enclosed passageway leading down into the rock. Darkness surrounds you. You become aware of your own apprehension about this journey but are determined to continue.

Now, you see the way ahead is blocked. The path has ended before a wall in which is set the first gate to Irkalla. The door is constructed of obsidian, carved with ancient Sumerian script, and there appears to be no physical way to open it.

You know that in order to continue, and to reach Ereshkigal deep within Irkalla, you must now begin to remove your *me* (which can be jewellery, garments or other items of meaning to you). Become aware of what powers the first item you'll take off possesses, what it means to you, what it says about you. You know the sacrifice must be made.

Remove the item and place it at the foot of the gateway. Use your inner voice to create a strong tonal sound (if the location permits it, you can project your voice in reality at the same time). Direct this wall of sound towards the obsidian gate. Keep this up by increasing the strength of your tonal sound until, suddenly, the gate splits vertically in two and opens wide. Then fall silent both in body and in mind. You can now go forward on your journey.

Now your journey feels easier, as if the weight of the item you removed has been lifted from you. In some small way, you are different, changed. You continue to follow the downward path, which is like a descending ramp of polished slabs within a long, dark corridor. Your initial fears have transformed into an anxious curiosity. Your pace quickens, as does your breathing and heartbeat. You stare into the darkness and presently see a dim glow. Just ahead another obsidian gate now blocks the path. Burning torches stand to either side of it.

You must remove another of your *me*. This sacrifice is

more difficult than the first one, for this glamour is more important to you. But still you make it. As you do so, be aware of what this item means to you, says about you, how you need it to protect you, define you.

Once the item has been placed upon the path, use your voice again to project sound towards the polished obsidian door. Keep this up until it mysteriously disappears from view, so you're able to continue your journey. How the door disappears is up to you. It could simply vanish; it might disintegrate from the centre outwards, or it could rise upwards like a raised curtain. These and other methods will allow you to tackle each door in turn and penetrate the heart of Irkalla, deep within the earth.

Again, you feel as if a weight has been lifted from you, which you were unaware of before. You must repeat this process another five times before you can finally reach Ereshkigal's palace, being aware each time you remove a symbolic *me* of what each item means to you, how important it is to you, but also how you feel lighter, yet stronger, once it is gone.

You continue your journey, travelling downwards, deep into the mountains. You know now what you must do as every door or gate is reached. The path becomes steeper, narrower. You have to feel your way along it.

By the time you reach the sixth gate, you feel as if the person you are in the mundane world is disappearing. You are becoming pure essence, without construction, masks or deceits. You are both afraid and eager to discover what happens at journey's end.

Once you have passed through the sixth gate, you see a faint glow in the distance, which as you draw closer to it becomes brighter. You see it is a wall of flame. This is the last gate. You must now make the final sacrifice, the last vestige of your earthly shields and identity. You do so and simply walk naked through the flames, which feel cool to you and do not harm you.

Before you lies the entrance to Ganzir, Ereshkigal's palace. Pass through it. Beyond, you discover a vast structure, a place of shadows and torches, and immense chambers. You begin to explore it, drawn ever to its dark heart.

You can hear strange sounds that might be discordant music, or the cries of animals, vultures, and even the souls of the dead. Sometimes you might hear short, sharp bursts of laughter or weeping. They come and go as if part of the fabric of the place. They never frighten you. You stay calm and focused throughout the whole ordeal.

Eventually you find your way to the inner chamber, the throne room of Ereshkigal. Here she sprawls indolently upon a huge obsidian throne, carved with astounding creatures, and strewn with animal furs. She stands as you approach her, a woman around seven feet high. She is dressed in dark robes, with an elaborate headdress. Her bare arms and neck are adorned with serpents of gold. She appears fierce and cold. You know you're not welcome here for she sees in you her traitorous sister, Inanna.

Tell Ereshkigal who you are and why you have sought her out. Explain clearly that you wish to learn her mysteries. You have surrendered the appropriate tokens at each gate. You are naked before her.

Show the goddess you are not afraid of her, in your posture and the strength and the sureness of your voice. Do not falter, for she will respect you if you remain calm and strong.

She says: 'If you seek my mysteries, sibling, will you consent to hang upon a hook, here in my palace and contemplate the mysteries of your own life?'

You give your consent. You are not here to trick or betray her, only to learn and to understand the symbols behind the myths.

Ereshkigal waves her hand and suddenly you find

yourself hanging upon the wall of her throne room, your body bound tightly by rope. This doesn't pain you – in fact, you are calm and at ease. Your physical body is unimportant during this transformative process. Surrender yourself, and see what thoughts fill your mind. Contemplate how the glamours you create to protect yourself, and how you swathe your being with them, are inessential to you. The kernel of your essence, once free of the constructions of an earthly existence and all the defences you've fashioned in order to live a comfortable life, is far stronger than petty human concerns. The glamours mean nothing here. They mean nothing to your magical progression. Ego and vanity only hold you back. They are lies and deceits. If you have any vestiges of the *me* attached to you, release them now.

Suddenly, you find you are standing on the floor of the throne room once more, before Ereshkigal. She nods to you, indicating she approves of your conduct.

She says: 'When you leave this place, leave your glamours behind. What exists within you is far more formidable than any meaningless bauble or frippery. Your own inner strength will clothe you in splendour.'

You may spend some further time conversing with Ereshkigal if you wish. When you are ready to leave the pathworking, return to the garden by visualising the central tree clearly. This is your beacon and your guide. Be aware that a part of yourself remained there while you were travelling. It was and is your anchor. Return to that part of yourself simply by thinking this. You find yourself standing beneath the tree, feeling calm and refreshed. Return to normal consciousness and open your eyes.

Hel by Danielle Lainton

Hel
Queen of the Dead

From the east comes Hrym with shield held high;
In giant-wrath does the serpent writhe;
O'er the waves he twists, and the tawny eagle
Gnaws corpses screaming; Naglfar is loose.
O'er the sea from the north there sails a ship
With the people of Hel, at the helm stands Loki;
After the wolf do wild men follow,
And with them the brother of Byleist goes.

From *Völuspá*, a poem of the *Poetic Edda*,
(translated by Henry Adams Bellows, 1923)

Hel is a Norse goddess who appears in many of the old stories found in the Eddas and other historical epics. She was the queen of the Underworld, which shared her name as Helheim. If someone was described as 'going to Hel', it meant they had died. Different forms of her name include Hella, Helya and Halja. Hel is generally thought to mean 'concealed' or 'hidden'. Helheim is a realm of the dead populated only by those who died of old age or sickness or were not considered worthy by the gods to go to any better afterlife, i.e. they had died a 'straw death' rather than death in physical combat.

The legends say Hel was a daughter of the trickster god, Loki, and a female *jötunn* (or giant) named Angrboða. She had two siblings: the wolf Fenrir, and the Serpent of Midgard, Jörmungandr. The other gods were suspicious of these three children, primarily because their father and mother were renowned for their unpredictable and troublesome natures. No doubt these peculiar offspring would only bring chaos and upset. Odin called for the three to be brought before him and then administered his uncompromising justice. The serpent Jörmungandr was tossed into the ocean, the wolf Fenrir was bound, and Hel was thrown into Niflheim, the World of Darkness, and one of the nine worlds of the Norse belief system. Here, Odin gave Hel authority over the nine worlds in the role of a goddess of death. He decreed that she must provide a home and sustenance to the dead who were sent to her realm.

In the old tales, Hel was said to possess a vast mansion with towering walls, called Nagrindr, (the 'corpse fence'), and enormous gates. She possessed a great hall known as Éljúðnir, which meant 'icy cold'. She had many servants under her dominion, foremost of which were Ganglati and Ganglöt, male and female attendants, whose names meant 'lazy walker' in ancient Norse. Within her hall, Hel had a dish named Hunger and a knife named Famine. The threshold to the hall was known as 'Stumbling Block' and the couch upon which she slept was 'Sick Bed'. The drapes or curtains of her domain were known as 'Gleaming-Bale', indicating misfortune.

Hel's realm was guarded by a monstrous hound named Garmr, who resided in a cave, and who set up a racket of howling every time someone approached his mistress's realm – whether that was a new potential resident or else some brave hero or heroine arriving to seek audience with Hel. Garmr's howling alerted the serpent Níðhöggr, or Nidhogg ('Malice Striker'), that some new souls might be arriving, upon whose blood it might suck. Níðhöggr mainly spent its time gnawing at the roots of the world tree Yggdrasil, which penetrated into Helheim.

The Underworld queen was described as having a dour and gloomy countenance yet was also fierce in appearance. She was half blue (or black), perhaps denoting rotting flesh, and half the colour of living, healthy flesh. In modern paganism, Hel is sometimes depicted as being half beautiful woman with a pale skin, and half skeleton, or decomposing corpse. In character she was generally presented as cruel and cold.

Hel is also somewhat tenuously connected with the weird ship, Naglfar. This vessel is comprised of the fingernails and toenails of the dead – the word Naglfar means 'nail ship'. It's said that when Ragnarok, the end of the world, takes place, an army of the dead will rise up against the gods. The dead, in this instance, must surely be those considered 'less honourable' than the noble souls who died in combat and ended up in more respectable afterlifes, such as residing in the halls of Valhalla or the goddess Freya's fields of Fólkvangr. The dead of Helheim will swarm upon the Naglfar, which will be released from its moorings by the upheaval. The Naglfar will act as a ferry, transporting this vast army to the battlefields. This seems to suggest that the Naglfar is capable of sailing upon elements other than water. When the dire time draws due, the Naglfar will be captained by a giant named Hrym, and beside him will stand Loki, Hel's father, and her uncle Býleistr. Because the dead are her people, Hel will no doubt play a prominent part in the events of Ragnarok, if the powerful gods can't keep her, Helheim's denizens, and her fearsome relatives under control.

Meeting Hel
Caroline Wise

Begin the pathworking by entering the Garden of Gateways. To meet with Hel, you will go into the northern part of the garden. Take the appropriate exit from the centre of the garden and follow the path to the northern cave.

You emerge from the cave into an icy-cold bleak landscape, on a path in a valley between two round hills. The path is stony, and the light is twilight-dim. Bats circle above. Your breath clouds white from the chilling air. You look down and see you are dressed in a thick wool cloak, fastened at the shoulder by an ornate pin of silver, jet, and quartz. You feel you are standing outside of linear time, at a place where millennia overlap.

You become aware of the smell of the sea; sharp, tangy, of salt and seaweed, as you tread the path towards the sound of waves lapping a shore. You arrive at a beach of a small crescent-shaped bay on the far side of the hills. As you watch, mesmerised by the rhythm of the waves rolling in, you are startled by the sudden caw of ravens. Looking up, you see the ravens are flying in from the sea, as outriders, heralding a strange ship. The figurehead of the ship is of a giant woman, with a stern face that appears half black and half white. Her long white hair is carved in a way that seems to flow from the prow down the hull, to merge with the sea.

As the ship nears, you see it is made of bones and finger nails. It comes to a halt and a rock jetty is revealed by the receding tide. From the bone ship, a gang-plank appears, and a statuesque figure rides out on a three-legged horse. In spite of this strangeness, the horse doesn't break stride with its weird gait. On its back rides a woman; half black and half bone-white, like her figurehead. Behind her follow howling wolves and dogs. She holds forth a bone-white sceptre with a skull atop. It intrigues you and sends an atavistic chill up your spine to your brain, evoking fleeting images of those who lived too many aeons ago to grasp.

You know that this is Hel.

You feel no fear as Hel bids you travel with her. She pulls you up behind her on her horse.

As she charges across the land of hills and valleys, fords and fields, you observe Hel, with a sweep of her sceptre, gathering the souls of the ancient dead. This includes those on their death beds – farmers, mothers dying in childbirth, housewives, fishers, prostitutes, blacksmiths, bar maids, servants. As Hel approaches, they seem relieved, and appear to give up their souls willingly to her. Their eyes close on lifeless bodies. Their spirits rise up in in raggedy shrouds, following Hel.

She tells you in your mind: 'I am the fetch of death. I catch them at the seconds between life and their earthly end.'

Your journey quickens now, as you ride down a steep slope towards a cave opening. You descend a stone passage, lit by a glow of an unknown source. Veins of jet and quartz and silver are revealed, glinting in the grey rock.

At the base of this slope, you enter Niflheim, the realm of Hel. At the centre of a vast chamber, the roots of an immense tree twist. This is Yggdrasil, the tree of life, in its lower world aspect, and you see at its base a coiled dragon, which has a weather eye on you. The walls of the chamber are formed of hissing snakes, their venom falling like rain, making an impressive living tapestry.

There are nine arched openings from the chamber, and you wonder what lies beyond them.

Hel dismounts and bids you follow her. She ascends a stone throne, holding her sceptre. The strange horse stands aside, and you hear the pawing of its hooves on the ground, and the occasional snort.

She beckons you towards her. She shows you the sceptre and bids you study it. You see is made of a giant's spinal cord. You touch it and see visons of a line of people going back behind you, your ancestors – and then, deeper back in time, a giant race, which you know are your ancestor's ancestors. You feel part of a vast chain, and your place in it, which gives a sense of security and continuity, rather than fear.

Hel speaks:

'This is the castle of the dead. Of the long forgotten and the never remembered. Those who were not mourned, who lie in unmarked graves, or whose graves lie unattended and overgrown. Of those who lived seemingly unremarkable lives, but whose contributions to the great scheme of the universe were just as important as the warrior. For all those who die of sickness or old age, of overwork and poverty, of famine and exhaustion, I take them as my due. I give them honour that no one hears. I send them to one of the nine worlds of death, through these doorways around me, but you will not enter such a realm today, now is not your time. You are here to understand my role. For my dish is Hunger, my knife is Famine, and my throne is the Sick Bed of the life lived and the inevitable death. Take from me now the gifts of my domain, that you may link with your ancestors, that they may have immortality through your imaginings.' Hel hands you a shining black jet scrying mirror, and two white quartz stones.

'These are the stones of my domain – jet, made from

the decaying tree matter of two hundred thousand years ago, trees your ancestor's ancestors saw growing. You may see visions of them and commune with in this mirror. Take also these quartz pebbles, once used as grave goods for your unknown ancestors. The secret is that when rubbed hard together, they create light, to light the way for the dead. When you do this, you will aid passing souls. The third gift is two silver coins. Leave instruction for these to be placed on your own eyelids when the time comes, and I will know you as my initiate and claim you and honour your life.'

You look up from the gifts, and see that Hel is no longer present. The horse is silent, and the dragon appears to sleep, and the dogs and wolves no longer howl. It is time to leave this realm, with all the knowledge you have gathered. You start to ascend the stone passage towards the middle world where you entered.

When you are ready to depart, return to the garden by visualising the central tree clearly. This is your beacon and your guide. Be aware that a part of yourself remained there while you were travelling. It was and is your anchor. Return to that part of yourself simply by thinking this. You find yourself standing beneath the tree, feeling calm and refreshed. Return to normal consciousness and open your eyes.

Tomb Painting of Nephthys with Anubis

Nephthys
Lady of Dark and Light

Maggie Jennings

*'I've been searching for the daughter of the Devil himself.
I've been searching for an angel in white.
I've been waiting for a woman who's a little of both,
And I can feel her but she's nowhere in sight.'*

from *One of These Nights* by The Eagles

The above verse of this song, made famous by The Eagles, could have been written for Nephthys, a member of the Great Ennead of Heliopolis – a royal family of gods. She was the dark sister of the Egyptian goddess Isis, married to Set, the brother and murderer of Osiris. Her name is believed to mean 'Lady of the Temple Enclosure', referring to her role in the funerary rites of pharaohs, over which she presided with her sister Isis.

*'Ascend and descend; descend with Nephthys,
sink into darkness with the Night-bark.
Ascend and descend; ascend with Isis,
rise with the Day-bark.'*

Pyramid Text PT 222

The quote above suggests that in some ways Nephthys was regarded as the 'dark' sister (in this instance associated with the sun's journey through the night), while Isis is the 'bright' sister associated with daylight. This is not meant to suggest that Nephthys and Isis should be regarded as opposites, but rather both are essential parts of the eternal cycle of life and death.

Nephthys is the epitome of the dark feminine, mysterious and deceptive, illusive and beautiful, the *femme fatale* of the Egyptian pantheon. As the wife of Set, the god of disorder and violence, she might have been attracted to ruthlessness and cruelty, but in *'The Pyramid Texts'* she is also spoken of as a protector of the dead, a goddess who represented the experience of death as Isis represents the experience of life. Yet she was also described as a nurse and guardian for Isis's son, Horus, as well as being the 'nurse' of the reigning pharaoh. Additionally, she was connected to the secret depths of the ocean, unseen but nonetheless powerful. Her story speaks of all these aspects.

As the queen of sorcery and shadows, she was usually only defined in relation to her divine family and there was no cult specifically dedicated to her worship.

Isis, Nephthys, Set and Osiris were siblings. Isis was married to Osiris and Nephthys was married to Set. Set was filled with hatred and jealousy of his brother, so he conspired with his friends and tricked Osiris, eventually killing him and dismembering his body. Isis was distraught and spent years searching for the pieces. Nephthys sprang to the aid of her sister and assisted in finding and reassembling the missing parts of Osiris. She also protected Horus, the son of Isis and Osiris, after Isis magically managed to conceive by enlivening Osiris' remembered corpse.

However, Nephthys also has a dark side. She was credited with enabling the pharaoh to see 'that which is hidden by moonlight.' As a goddess of the darkening moon, people believed she lived on the boundary of the parched desert regions and personified the qualities of hidden desire and secrecy. These qualities prove very useful, as after Osiris' murder and dismemberment by Set, Nephthys helps her sister find and hide the missing pieces. This enables Isis to magically restore him and conceive Horus, who grows up to avenge his father. One story tells us that when Nephthys herself wanted to conceive a child, she was unable to do so with her husband, as he was sterile. His domain was the barren desert, harsh and arid, in which nothing could grow. So she disguised herself as Isis and lay with Osiris, leading to the birth of her son, Anubis. In one version of the myth, Set discovers his wife's infidelity, and this is what initiates his hatred for Osiris. So, Nephthys deceived her brother and her husband and possibly also her sister, although there is a hint in some of the stories that Isis may have helped her sister to disguise herself in order to seduce Osiris.

Nephthys has a secret love for peace and order. In the stories, Nephthys seems quite happy to live quietly with Osiris and Isis in the Duat, having left her husband. After reading the myths, I feel that her deceptions ultimately work in the service of truth and love. It's as if she feels there is a higher pattern and order in the world that she needs to follow, which redeems her apparently selfish actions. Her deceptions around the conception of her son, Anubis, result in the creation of a god who presides over the dead, weighing their hearts against the feather of truth. As the son of both the dark and the light, he has the gift of perfect calibration. With Isis, Nephthys represents the cosmic balance in the cycles of night and day, darkness and light, life and death.

The unconscious forces represented by Nephthys may lead us to do things that are against the standards set by society, but which, in the end, can have a positive outcome.

Meeting Nephthys
Maggie Jennings

Begin the pathworking by entering the Garden of Gateways. To meet with Nephthys, you will go into the western part of the garden.

The air is cold and crystal clear. The sky is white with low clouds. It is late autumn, and the branches of the tree are bare of apples. You look down at your feet and see that you are standing amongst broken twigs and dead leaves.

You turn to the west, as now you are going to enter the realm of the element of water. Walk towards the gap in the hedge and find yourself once more on the rising pathway set between ornamental rockeries. Walk carefully along the path. The evergreen plants along the path are dark green, but they look untidy and are interspersed with dead leaves and grasses, the lush growth of summer now a distant memory. A cold wind is blowing, and you shiver slightly, wrapping your arms around yourself for warmth. You hear the stones on the path scrunch beneath your feet.

After a while, you come across the stone portal and once more find yourself by the scrying pool. The water is dark and deep, and as you look at it, you feel yourself falling. Somehow you feel that you will not be harmed, and you let yourself slide into the water. It closes over your head and you feel as if you are submerged in a warm blanket. You also find that you can breathe. As you discover this surprising fact you open your eyes ... and find yourself on the bank of a river.

Dusk is approaching, but the air is still hot and sultry.

You are standing on a marshy green area, surrounded by tall papyrus plants, and the River Nile flows wide and deep before you.

You see a long, narrow boat moving through the water – it looks like it is made of woven reeds and has one square sail. The boat is coming towards you, and you can see the oarsmen's muscles ripple as they labour at propelling the vessel. In the centre of the boat is a small square structure and standing in front of it is a beautiful Egyptian woman, wearing a long black wig and a red dress, her head adorned by a strange tall headdress that represents a house and a basket. She carries an ankh, the Egyptian symbol of life.

You know that this is Nephthys riding upon the Barque of Night, who accompanies the sun god Ra into the Duat.

The boat comes to a halt in the reeds before you. Nephthys turns to you and holds out her hand. You sense that you are in no danger, so you wade through the shallow water to the boat, where one of the oarsmen helps you aboard.

Nephthys greets you and asks if you will travel with her into the realm of night.

You tell her you have come to learn her mysteries and will gladly go with her into the darkness.

The night comes down around you, until the boat floats through utter blackness. You sense you have passed from the mundane world into the Duat, the Underworld, the place where the dead reside before rebirth and where the sun rests at night.

In this place, Nephthys speaks to you of her functions, and how sometimes you must take action for the greater good, even if that action seems dubious at the time. You understand that all gods are beyond good and evil, simply representations of qualities and states. In Osiris we find growth and life, while Set represents the chaos of the desert storms, unpredictable and violent, even life-threatening. Our own lives are threatened with storms and yet there are always oases of calm and rest, of growth. Sometimes we must take action to ensure that peace and growth follow the storms, to maintain balance in the rhythms and cycles of life.

Talk with Nephthys about dilemmas and situations in your own life, the problems you've had to face and deal with. She might offer you advice or a symbolic gift or show you scenes that dramatise your experiences and help you understand them, perhaps offering different viewpoints.

The Duat instils within you a sense of silence and loneliness. Along the banks of the night river, in the shadows of the Duat, you see upon the shore many things that illuminate your understanding of the cycles in life, how there can be no light without dark, no luck without ill luck, no life without death. Everything changes and is subjective for the individual.

You might consider ways in which you have gone against society's norms and values in the past. Think about what you learned about yourself and others by doing this. See how you might have worked for the greater good through your choices and actions, even unconsciously, and that this helped you realise your own strengths and limitations.

You glance at Nephthys and wonder at her quiet serenity. You realise that she is a survivor, and how important that quality is. Spend some time communing with her.

The boat now approaches the dawn. You can see a faint rosy light in the distance and know that soon you'll return to your own reality. The boat approaches the shore and as the light strengthens, you see you're back where you started, standing at the side of the Nile. The image of the boat is fading as the light increases. You see Nephthys raise her hand in a last farewell, then the sun rises above the horizon and the boat vanishes.

Behind you, you hear voices, talking excitedly, and turn to see a gracious temple behind you, set amid lush vegetation and palm trees. People are emerging from this temple and now call to you to join them. They represent life and light, as Nephthys represented the silence and darkness of the Underworld. While your contemplation in the Duat brought you knowledge, now is the time to celebrate your enlightenment, beneath the sun.

Spend some time with the people around you, celebrating the journey of life, represented by Isis riding upon the Barque of Day. Perhaps you even glimpse a glowing image of her boat upon the Nile. Secure and at rest, you forgive yourself for any past mistakes. With that forgiveness comes a sense of release, and with that feeling you see a bird, a large kite, flying away from you into the lightening sky. You realise that the kite is Nephthys, and you send her your thanks for the insights you have received.

When you are ready to depart, return to the garden by visualising the central tree clearly. This is your beacon and your guide. Be aware that a part of yourself remained there while you were travelling. It was and is your anchor. Return to that part of yourself simply by thinking this. You find yourself standing beneath the tree, feeling calm and refreshed. Return to normal consciousness and open your eyes.

Further Journeys

The framework of the pathworkings created for this book can be utilised to investigate any deity or supernatural entity. You can start with the myths and history surrounding the being you're interested in and the people who venerated them in the past.

Investigating different sources, such as myths and fairy tales, ancient history and the religious beliefs of different cultures will be rewarding. Exploring these subjects is a journey in itself, as you wander the winding paths of information, interpretations and ideas you'll find by browsing the internet, poring through old books, visiting museums and art galleries, or watching films and documentaries. We recommend all of these activities, so you expose yourself to more than one stream of influence.

A goddess, or any other entity you wish to explore, could consist of a meld of fact, need and belief. In their original forms, we can imagine how they were shaped to assist with specific predicaments at specific times. Our modern interpretations might be developed from an idea inspired by a desire, a dream, an emotion, a conversation with a friend, or a strong sensation in a special place. Our goddesses evolve constantly, shifting shape, eluding imprisonment in dogma and doctrine.

The powerful goddesses and feminine archetypes featured in this book represent a fraction of the vast number of deities and supernatural creatures that humankind have fashioned and believed in since consciousness awoke within them. The journeys, and the encounters, will never cease if there are explorers to find and walk the path.

About the Contributors

Andrew Collins is a science and history writer, and the author of books that challenge the way we perceive the past. They include *From the Ashes of Angels*, *Gods of Eden*, *Gateway to Atlantis*, *Tutankhamen: The Exodus Conspiracy* (co-authored with Chris Ogilvie Herald), *The Cygnus Mystery*, *Göbekli Tepe: Genesis of the Gods* and *The Cygnus Key: The Denisovan Legacy, Göbekli Tepe and the Birth of Egypt*. He is a co-founder of the quantum consciousness discipline of psychic questing. Andrew lives in Leigh-on-Sea, Essex. His website is www.andrewcollins.com

Storm Constantine has studied alternative beliefs and spirituality for over four decades. She has taught courses in the subject and has run groups devoted to it, including alternative methods of healing. As an internationally published author, she has produced over thirty novels and short story collections, and has also written nonfiction works, including *Bast and Sekhmet: Eyes of Ra* (with Eloise Coquio, Robert Hale, 1999), *Sekhem Heka* (Megalithica Books, 2008) and the three book *Grimoire Dehara* series (Megalithica Books, 2005, 2016, 2017), a pop culture magic system based on the spiritual beliefs of the androgynous Wraeththu, a race Storm created when she was a teenager, which she has written about extensively ever since, and who have appeared in three trilogies and seven anthologies. The first Wraeththu trilogy (*The Enchantments of Flesh and Spirit* 1988, *The Bewitchments of Love and Hate* 1989, and *The Fulfilments of Fate and Desire* 1990 published by Futura Macdonald) was described as ground-breaking when it first appeared for its exploration of gender and authentic practices of magic. Storm continues to weave her magical experience into her fiction, both in short stories and full-length novels. She is the founder of Immanion Press/Megalithica Books and is its senior editor. She lives in the Midlands of England with her husband and four cats. She can be found on Facebook, where she posts news about her own work and other Immanion Press titles, and her web site can be found at stormconstantine.co.uk

Deborah Cartwright studied philosophy and is a published author on self-development and esoteric psychology with Storm Constantine. She was the co-founder of The Luciferian Society in 2016, which is an LHP and philosophy network for light-bearers and existential self-knowledge seekers and continues to administer it.

She is best known for her work with authors Andrew Collins, Graham Phillips and Paul Weston in the movement known as psychic questing and has inspired many of their books on this genre of earth mysteries and historical investigation.

Deborah is also a keen landscape photographer, who captures images and creates photo art from the story of ancient places of power and magic within their landscape setting. This work has been published in books, and on her website www.earthquestphotography.com

Maggie Jennings has been interested in the spiritual path for many years, having learned how to read Tarot at the age of 12 and escaping from PE lessons at school to read books about ancient civilisations in the school library. After teaching in Further Education for 15 years, she qualified as an aromatherapy practitioner. Maggie has also undergone two years of priestess training based on the Egyptian magical traditions. She now runs a holistic shop in Stafford, which is also a recognised VTCT training centre; where Maggie teaches aromatherapy, reiki, Tarot, crystals and other magical courses. She is currently working on a book tracing the origins of Tarot back to Ancient Egypt via early mystical traditions.

Danielle Lainton is a freelance artist, amateur aerialist, occasional actress and owner of a bespoke cake company, with a propensity for the strange and the macabre. She has been working with Immanion Press for over ten years in one capacity or another, starting as a cover artist and illustrator and, more recently, she has added editing and proof-reading to her repertoire.

Richard Ward is a researcher and writer on esoteric themes. He has studied the occult for over thirty years, and over the last twenty years his work has been published in a wide variety of journals and anthologies. These include essays in periodicals such as *Talking Stick*, *the Cauldron*, *Pagan Dawn*, *Starfire*, and *Lovecraft Studies*. He has also been featured in a small number of book anthologies – *Devoted* (Scarlet Imprint 2008), *At the Crossroads* (Scarlet Imprint 2012), and *Sounds Beyond Meaning* (Von Zos 2014). His first full length book, *Echoes from the Primal Grimoire*, was published in 2016 by Von Zos.

Richard still lives in his native Essex where he sells second-hand books on esoteric subjects through his website manmythandmagic.com, and continues to pursue his occult interests, particularly with regard to traditional English folk magic and African traditional religious systems.

Caroline Wise has been exploring the many goddesses of the world since the late 70s. She was administrator for the Fellowship of Isis for many years in the 1990s, a large international endeavour concerned with restoring the Divine Feminine to the world. During this time, she taught weekly classes on the goddesses and trained priestesses. A former owner of The Atlantis Bookshop in London, Caroline has contributed to many books about the goddesses, including *Naming the Goddess* (Moon Books, 2014) and *Bast and Sekhmet*, by Storm Constantine and Eloise Coquio (Robert Hale, 1999), and books about women pioneers in the magical revival. Throughout the 90s, she presented conferences on the Goddess for the FOI, and also the Wildwood Conferences, restoring the link between folklore and earth mysteries and modern paganism. She compiled the book *Finding Elen: The Quest for Elen of the Ways*, (Amazon CreateSpace, 2015) about a lost, antlered goddess. With John Matthews she is co-editor of *The Secret Lore of London* (Hodder and Stoughton, 2016). She runs goddess days and workshops, and speaks in Germany, Italy and the USA on the subject. Her website is www.starofelen.com

SHE: Primal Meetings with the Dark Goddess

Collector's Limited Edition

A special hardback edition of this book, with wrap around jacket, in a numbered limited edition of 99 copies. This title is only available direct from Immanion Press, as every copy will be numbered by hand.

The collector's edition of 'SHE' includes a bonus section – 'Goddesses of Greater Darkness', featuring Lyssa: Mistress of Madness, Melinoë: The Night Terror and Kalma: The Odour of the Grave.

With cover art by Danielle Lainton and additional illustrations to accompany the pathworkings, this book will be a rare addition to your library. ISBN: 978-1-912241-07-1 Price: £29.99

Email orders@immanion-press.com to enquire about availability.

www.immanion-press.com

Pop Culture Magic from Megalithica Books

Grimoire Dehara

Taking pop culture magic to a fine focus, this series of books explores and expands upon the magical system created by Storm Constantine for her novels and stories of the Wraeththu – a race of androgynous beings, the next stage of human evolution, who inhabit a future earth.

Richly illustrated by the artist Ruby, these volumes introduce the deities of this system, the Dehara themselves, and provide an innovative approach to Neopagan practices, which involves the exploration of the androgynous nature of the soul.

These ground-breaking grimoires are essential additions to the library of any experimental practitioners of magic looking for something new to explore, as well as enthusiasts of Storm Constantine's work who are interested in the background to the magic within the novels.

Grimoire Dehara: Kaimana 978-1-905713-55-4. Pbk £10.99 $19.99
Grimoire Dehara: Ulani 978-0-9932371-8-8. Pbk £10.99 $19.99
Grimoire Dehara: Nahir Nuri 978-0-912241-02-6. Pbk £10.99, $19.99

Also available in a numbered, limited edition hardback set. See our web site for further details

www.immanion-press.com

Recent Titles from Megalithica Books

Zodiac of the Gods by Eden Crane

A new interpretation of the Egyptian Dendera Zodiac, this book explores character analysis for each sign, revealing your relationship with the deity presiding over your month of birth. The book also offers a primer for Egyptian magic, focusing upon the deities of the year. The vivid pathworkings enable you to connect with these ancient gods and goddesses, and work with their energy to influence and improve your life, helping you realise your goals and desires. ISBN: 978-1-912241-03-3 Price: £11.99, $16.50

The Heart of the Elder by Lillith ThreeFeathers & Joy Wedmedyk

Elders are a vital component of pagan and neopagan traditions. This book offers all you need to know about them. Learn how to identify, meet, and work with Elders and the distinguishing characteristics of great Elders. This book teaches how to originate and maintain meaningful relationships with your Elders and unique teaching styles. It illumines the mysterious benefits of training with Elders and includes amazing stories of life-changing events. ISBN: 978-1-912241-04-0 Price: £9.99, $12.99

The Elemental Magic Workbook by Soror Velchanes

A complete course in elemental magic, providing a solid foundation for future independent work. Explore the nature of each element, how it impacts your life and how you may harness it for personal benefit. Perform elemental rites inspired by various magical tradition, and also develop and perform your own rites. Previous magical experience is helpful but is not required. Everyone is welcome to work with the elements! ISBN: 978-1-912241-05-7 Price: £11.99, $16.50

www.immanion-press.com